Bongology

Bongology

n. The art of creating **35** of the world's most Bongtastic marijuana ingestion devices

CHRIS STONE

TEN SPEED PRESS
Berkeley

Copyright © 2010 by
Elephant Book Company Limited

Illustrations copyright © 2010 by
Elephant Book Company Limited

Published in the United States by Ten Speed Press, an
imprint of the Crown Publishing Group, a division of
Random House, Inc., New York, by arrangement with
Elephant Book Company Limited, 35 Fournier Street,
London E1 6QE, United Kingdom

www.crownpublishing.com
www.tenspeed.com

Ten Speed Press and the Ten Speed colophon are registered
trademarks of Random House, Inc.

Editorial Director: Will Steeds
Project Editors: Laura Ward, Clarissa Dolphin
Cover and Interior Design: Lindsey Johns
Illustrator: Robert Brandt
Bong Maker: Paul Malden
Copy editors: Karen Stein, Pandora Palmer-Edwards
Production: Robert Paulley
Color Reproduction:
Modern Age Repro House Ltd., Hong Kong

Ten Speed Press Editor: Lisa Westmoreland

Library of Congress Cataloging-in-Publication Data

Stone, Chris.
  Bongology: the art of creating 35 of the world's most
bongtastic marijuana devices / by Chris Stone.
        p. cm.
  Summary: "A manual for today's DIY smoker, featuring 35
ingenious projects for crafting unique bongs from watering cans,
traffic cones, pineapples, and more"—Provided by publisher.
1.   Handicraft. 2.   Smoking paraphernalia—Design and
construction. 3.   Marijuana. I. Title.
  TT157.S825 2010
  745.5—dc22

                                        2009036621

ISBN 978-1-58008-043-9

Printed in China

10 9 8 7 6 5 4 3 2 1

First Edition

BONGOLOGY

Contents

Introduction

For today's smoker who is bored with the standard doobie, there is a galaxy of gadgets that can be used to get high. Bongs, chillums, hookahs, bubblers, vaporizers, and pipes come in an assortment of shapes and sizes, materials, and designs. Just take a look on the World Wide Web—it's a veritable Aladdin's cave of smoking toys. Whether you want a discreet pipe disguised as a pen for covert smoking or to roar away unashamedly on a—wait for it—Osama bin Laden bong, you can be sure that some merchandiser somewhere has got you covered.

However, all these contraptions have one thing in common. These toys will hit you in the pocket—in fact some wonderfully ornate bongs retail for upward of $300 (£170). Sure, they look great, but if you're like me then you probably want to save your hard-earned cash for more important things—namely, weed.

Bongology offers you the best of both worlds—the joy and creativity associated with the use of bongs, hookahs, and other smoking contraptions but at minimal cost. In the following pages, you, the budding bongologist, will discover thirty-five devices to make and smoke. Some are remarkably easy to build and require little more than a plastic bottle, a knife, a pen, and some putty. Other projects are more involved (the pièce de résistance being the

DISCLAIMER It is a criminal offense in the United States and in many other countries, punishable by imprisonment and/or fines, to cultivate, possess, or supply cannabis. You should therefore understand that this book is intended for private amusement and not intended to encourage you to break the law.

✹ ✹ ✹ ✹ ✹...........**All the bongs, pipes, and hookahs in this book are rated from one to five in the following categories:**

HIT POWER: ....The potency of the bong, pipe, or hookah—the greater the number of leaves shown, the more stoned you will get.

FREAKY FACTOR: ......Indicates the uniqueness and complexity of the shape and design of the bong, pipe, or hookah.

SMOOTHNESS:............How the smoking device feels and tastes when smoked—the more leaves shown, the smoother the smoke.

BUILDIN' TIME:.........How long (in minutes) the bong, pipe, or hookah takes to construct.

FAB—see page 112). But all utilize equipment that is readily available in your home or can be bought cheaply from your local garden center, hardware store, or grocery store.

For instance, the average teapot or teakettle makes a perfect bong with very few modifications; those with a heartier appetite might like to use a watering can. A small piece of aluminum foil, a matchbox, or a set of fire bellows each makes a great pipe. A mini liquor bottle can be made into a vaporizer. Armed with a traffic cone and a length of vinyl hose, you can make a stupendous hookah.

So, without further ado, let's begin your bongology training.

Chris Stone

chapter 1

BONG BASICS

"They sailed away for a year and a day
To the land where the bong-tree grows"

Edward Lear, *The Owl and the Pussycat* (1871)

Tempting though it may be to get your mouth over the nearest chamber and start firing up, before you start down the long road to bongology greatness, take a moment to learn about your craft. The more you understand the anatomy of bongs, pipes, and hookahs, the better prepared you will be to build your own shining example.

Getting Started

If you're reading this, I thank you. I mean it. I know you've probably just picked this book up from the store and you want to skip straight to the "good parts"—making smoking toys and getting high. But before you start raiding the shelves at your local hardware store, you'll want to learn how bongs, hookahs, and pipes work. I don't want this to be like a high school class, but paying a little attention now will help you to make the best bong possible and maintain it in the correct way. After all, do you know exactly how to use the "carb"? How often you should change the water? The benefits of a pipe screen? Read on, Grasshopper.

Why use bongs, pipes, and hookahs?

Not everyone is a fan of smoking contraptions. Plenty of stoners prefer joints. They wax lyrical about the art involved in rolling a nice fat cone and the joy of passing it among their friends. Sure, I like a joint as much as the next pothead—I certainly wouldn't pass on one that was going around the room—but joints have one crushing disadvantage: they're incredibly wasteful.

Efficiency

A joint is always burning, of course, and, unless you've got a manic puffer in your circle, much of that smoke ends up drifting into the atmosphere. If you grow your own buds you may be able to afford such carelessness, but many stoners pay big bucks for their weed, literally to watch it go up in smoke.

Bongs, bubblers, and pipes have a special advantage. Namely, the size of a "bowl" is far smaller than the volume of a joint, because it's intended to provide one or two hits for a single person—not twenty or more tokes for a bunch of guys, as is the case with the joint.

Cool, man

Joints are also much harsher on your lungs than bongs, bubblers, and hookahs are. While a few joint rollers use filters on their creations, nothing compares with the filtration effect of water. Not only does water cool the smoke, but it actually removes harmful impurities, too. (See "Water matters" on page 16.)

MATERIALS

There's a wide variety of containers and materials that you can use in making a bong, pipe, or hookah, so make sure they will be safe.

PLASTIC: Toughened plastic and acrylic sold in hardware stores is fine. PVC and flammable plastics are less so.

GLASS: Tempered glass is ideal, but beware of cheap store-bought bongs that can accidentally shatter. The best materials to use are chemistry supplies because they are designed to be airtight and to withstand high temperatures.

METALS: Stems and bowls made from aluminum, copper, and brass are fine. Stay away from any metal whose properties could leach into the water.

CLAY: Clay is great for bongs, not least because it can be molded into any shape you want. Just don't go to pottery class to learn how!

Bongs, Bubblers, and Hookahs

As we've learned, bongs come in all shapes and sizes, but the principle is always the same—to filter impurities from the smoke you inhale, and to cool that smoke, by first passing it through water. You are probably familiar with a bong's general appearance, but in case you are new to the world of bongs let's start at the beginning.

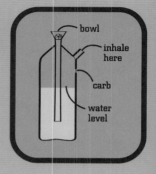

Anatomy of a bong

Bongs operate on a compression system, which sounds complex but really just has to do with being air- and watertight. Bongs are typically formed by a hollow vertical cylinder (the "tube" or "chamber") made of plastic, tempered glass, or metal with a diameter of about 4 inches (10 cm). This tube is closed at the bottom end and open at the top. Near the base of the tube, there's an integrated hollow stem, somewhat shorter and narrower than the main tube, which juts out at an angle of around 45 degrees. At the free end of this stem sits a "bowl."

The bowl is very much the business end of any bong. It's a small, conical-shaped piece of metal that houses the weed or hash. In some bongs the bowl is removable, but it's always substantially narrower at the bottom end. There's a very simple and practical reason for this—it prevents the mix from falling through the bottom of the bowl into the stem, further aided by the use of a pipe screen (see page 20).

About midway up the tube, usually on the side opposite the stem, is the "carb," also known variously as the "shotgun," "shottie," "shot hole," and "rush hole." On the face of it, it's nothing more than a small hole in the tube (with a diameter equivalent to that of the head of a large nail), and it isn't actually essential. However, it plays an important part in the smoking process after you've taken your hit.

Carb versus slide

Most bongs have a carb to clear the chamber of smoke, but carbs are not the only way. Some bongs feature removable stems, called "slides." A little gasket at the base of the stem creates an airtight seal whenever the slide is in the stem. The slide is pulled out of the stem by a small handle, allowing plain air to be sucked through the water, clearing the chamber.

TAKING A TOKE

Before you get started, let's go over the all-important technique for successful bongology.

- Place the top end of the tube under a tap and fill the bong with cold water (or other liquids—see page 17). It's vital to get this water level right: the water should cover the bottom of the stem but be below the level of the carb hole. Your bong should have a line marker on it to denote the optimum level.

- Load some mix into the bowl and pack it in tightly.

- Take hold of the bong with one hand about halfway up the tube, using your thumb to cover the carb hole.

- Holding a lighter or lit match in your free hand, take a couple of deep breaths and exhale deeply; then position your mouth inside the open end of the tube (ensuring it is airtight).

- Light the bowl and start inhaling until the flame is drawn into the mix and the mix is alight. Inhale steadily until the bowl is emptied.

- Take your thumb off the carb hole to clear the excess smoke from the tube.

- Load up the bowl again, pass it to your neighbor, and settle back to enjoy the effects.

Blowin' the bong

Blowing the bong is the cardinal sin of bongology. But we've all done it, and if you're a novice it'll probably happen several times before you get the hang of it. This faux pas happens when you exhale into the mouthpiece at any point during the hit. If you breathe out with any discernible force, the water will be forced up the stem and into the bowl. Once you've blown, the best you can hope for is that the water has merely dampened the mix—which in itself is a terrible waste of weed, but at least there's no lasting damage. The worst-case scenario is a jet of burned sludge and disgusting-smelling water landing on your new carpet. In the immortal words of Cypress Hill, "Home skillet, there's water inside don't spill it / It smells like shit on the carpet." Needless to say, the more stoned you are, the more likely you are to mess up. Repeat offenders should be made to drink the bong water.

HOT ROCKS

If a member of your smoking circle is prone to blowing the bong (put your hands up, you know who you are!) it's far safer to pack the bowl with weed rather than hash. Burning resin is more resistant to water than grass is and the last thing you want is "hot rocks" (small, flaming nuggets of hash) spraying around the room. Alternatively, make sure you always smoke at your buddy's house instead of yours!

Anatomy of a bubbler

Bubblers are a relatively new creation, known for their bulbous shape, utilizing aspects of both pipes and bongs. Usually about the size of a large glass pipe, they draw smoke into their "bubble" and filter the smoke through water, like a bong. If you like the cooled effect of a hit from a bong but also the portability of a pipe, this could be the device for you.

mouthpiece

bowl

carb

Anatomy of a hookah

First used during the reign of emperor Akbar (1542–1605) in Mughal India, the hookah is the father of the bong. The modern principle of the "water-cooled pipe" is identical to the original, though the design and deployment may be different.

In keeping with its regal past, the hookah is grander, larger, and considerably more ornate than a bong. There are other key differences. Unlike with the bong, the metal or plastic mouthpiece is at the end of a long tube traditionally made of cord. A hookah often has two or more of these tubes so the stoner can

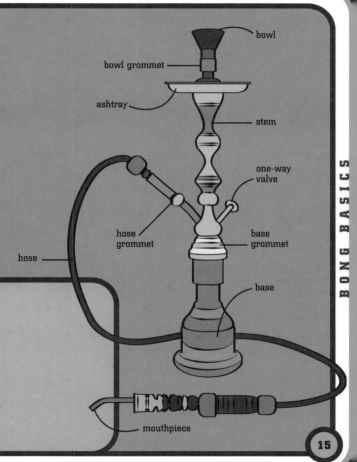

bowl

bowl grommet

ashtray

stem

one-way valve

hose grommet

base grommet

hose

base

mouthpiece

FRUITY FLAVORS

It is legal in the US for hookahs to be smoked with flavored tobacco instead of grass. Apple is a popular smoke but many other flavors are available. These include coconut, jasmine, vanilla, honey, mango, bubble gum, watermelon, mint, cherry, orange, raspberry, rose, apricot, chocolate, coffee, grape, peach, cola, and pineapple.

HOOKAH HABITS

In the Arab world, when the smoker is finished, either the hose is placed back on the table signifying that it is available, or it is handed from one user to the next—it's considered an insult to point the mouthpiece at the recipient, however. It's also common for the receiver to tap the previous smoker on the back of the hand while taking it, as a sign of friendship.

indulge simultaneously with friends. In that respect the hookah is a more sociable smoking toy than the bong. Of course, with so many puffers the bowl has a far greater capacity than the average bong. The mix (blend of tobacco and weed) sits at the bottom of the bowl with a layer of burning charcoal on top. Once ignited, the hookah will usually continue burning until the mix is finished—which can take up to, or more than, an hour.

Water matters

Water is clearly the vital ingredient of any bong, bubbler, or hookah, so before we leave the domain of water-based smoking devices, make note of the following:

Filtration

The temperature of the liquid is key. Iced or cold water cools the smoke.

The same effect is also achieved with boiling water—the steam moisturizes the smoke and removes the dryness and harshness.

Also important is the volume of water and depth of the chamber. The longer the smoke is in contact with the water, the greater the chance that it will soften the taste.

What's your flavor?

Plain water is not the only liquid that can be used in a bong. Using beer or liquor in a bong gives the smoke a tasty flavor. Fruit juice is an option although some may taste gross, depending on your palate; experiment with different flavors to find one you like. A squirt of fresh lemon or lime into the water will give a nice aroma.

Keep it fresh

If water is not changed frequently it will get stale. This will not only cause the bong or hookah to smell unpleasant but also negatively alter the taste of your bud. Depending on the size of your bong, I recommend changing the water either after every session (for small bongs) or once a month (for larger contraptions).

DIRTY HIGH

Contrary to popular myth, bong water doesn't retain THC, so there's no excuse for persisting with old water—it ain't gonna get you any more high.

Pipes & Vaporizers

The pipe is the simplest form of smoking contraption, and the earliest ones almost certainly preceded the bong in widespread use. Pipes can be made from ceramic, glass, wood, fruit, metal, or stone. Pipes are rarely longer than 8 inches (20 cm) and their capacity is small. Yet their size is also an advantage—pipes are portable and discreet (and sometimes edible, too).

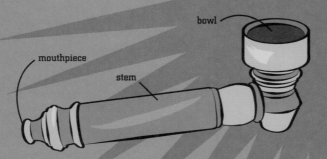

bowl

mouthpiece

stem

Anatomy of a pipe

All pipes feature a bowl, into which you load the grass, leading through a short hollow tube to a mouthpiece. Some metallic pipes come in two or more interchangeable parts that can be unscrewed to facilitate cleaning, and other pipes include a carb. Blown-glass pipes come in an array of wonderful designs, sometimes changing color with heat or through repeated use.

Anatomy of a vaporizer

While the bong and the hookah have long and storied traditions, the vaporizer is a more modern-day phenomenon. The effect it has had on the cannabis community is immense. In layman's terms, bongs burn the mix, giving off a toxic smoke full of by-products other than THC that the smoker does not necessarily want to inhale. The vaporizer, on the other hand, heats the mix in a partial vacuum so that the active compound in cannabis (THC) boils off into a vapor. The vapor is pretty much odorless and tasteless. So the stoner gets a top-quality hit without any of the harmful by-products. It's a win-win situation. The downside is that high-quality vaporizers are expensive. But you can make your own using a heating source such as a lightbulb, oil burner, or soldering iron. See page 104 for ideas.

removable top

mouthpiece

bowl

VAPORIZER HISTORY

While medicinal plants have been vaporized for centuries—the ancient Egyptians used heated stones—this process has only in recent years been developed for cannabis use. In 1993 Cherokee medicine man Eagle Bill began to develop his Shake & Vape, not dissimilar to the lightbulb vaporizer (see page 105). Today, firms in Canada, Germany, and the Netherlands are world leaders in the electric vaporizer market.

Tools of the Trade

Before you begin any construction it's important that you're aware of some basic tools you will require, from knives and scissors to adhesive. You don't want to get halfway through the building process only to discover that you're missing a vital component. Forewarned is forearmed, as a sensible nonsmoker once said.

The Poker

The poker is the universal tool for any cannabis enthusiast. It's vital to the art of joint rolling, packing down the end of the spliff, and generally cleaning up when a plump digit won't do. But it's equally important for bong and hookah use. Once the mix is alight, use your poker to counter any blockage and push the mix through the bowl. A metal implement is best—try a clean nail, a small screwdriver, or the awl attachment from a pocket knife.

Pipe screen

Also known as gauzes or filters, these screens are placed at the bottom of the bowl to ensure that only smoke—and not burned residue—gets through into the chamber. They tend not to be a feature of store-bought bongs, because the diameter of the opening of the bowl at the bottom end is very narrow. Pipe screens usually come in packs of five or ten and sell for about $1 (£0.58) in smoking-paraphernalia stores. (Screens are also available in the plumbing departments of hardware stores, where they are known as "aerator screens." Obviously not intended for bong use, these typically come in sizes larger than that of a bong bowl, but they can easily be cut down to size with a pair of scissors.)

SEALS

No, I'm not talking here about the sea mammal. Airtight and watertight seals are vital for any bong, pipe, or hookah. Use rubber washers and a glue gun for extra security.

Hardware tools

The level of tools required depends on the complexity of the bong being built and the resistance of the material used, but a pair of scissors and a standard craft or pocket knife are essential. For bongs made of acrylic tubing and/or Plexiglas, a small saw is required. Tools such as a selection of screwdrivers, awls, a hammer, and a drill are also very useful.

Adhesive

Some form of adhesive is required to make the most of the smoking contraptions in this book, from sticky putty to hold the bowl in place for the Earth Pipe (see page 32) to a glue gun for FAB (see page 112). In addition, it's advisable to have a variety of adhesives at your disposal to make running repairs.

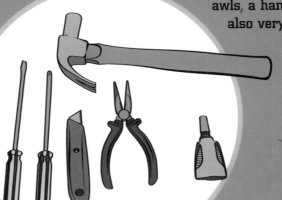

Bowls and downpipes

Bowls and downpipes (the stem that connects to the bowl) of various sizes are available at all good head shops at very good prices. They are used extensively in the smoking devices from chapter 3 onward, so it's worth investing in a few. Of course, you could make your own from brass nozzles and copper heating pipes.

Aluminum foil

A vital component of the cheaply constructed homemade bong, a small piece of foil, molded over a bong stem, makes a quick and disposable bowl. Once it's in place, prick the bottom several times with a pin to allow the smoke to draw through. Bear in mind that it does give off toxic vapor when burned, however, even though it is widely used. Where possible, a real bowl should be used instead.

Hardware store

It's not a tool in itself, of course, but the hardware store is a source of many useful bong basics. You probably recall weekend trips to the local hardware store from your childhood less than fondly. But, as you will quickly learn to appreciate, the hardware store is an unwitting friend of the bongologist. The plumbing department, in particular, is a veritable gateway to smoking joy. As well as pipe screens, the bowls used in all store-bought bongs are available, known at the hardware store as "brass nozzles." Plus, there's an abundance of vinyl hose (the hookah mouthpieces), and acrylic, brass, and steel tubing (which, cut to size, becomes the main body of a bong). Take a trip down there soon, and spend some time scanning the shelves to get inspired.

BE SUBTLE

Though there is clearly nothing illegal about purchasing large quantities of goods from a plumbing store, arriving at the cashier with a basket full of nozzles, plastic tubes, and pipe screens is likely to arouse suspicion in the mind of the ex-hippie working at the counter. The fewer people who know about your smoking activities, outside your circle of trust, the better. So use your judgment—perhaps make several trips over a period of a few days or purchase items from different stores. Not that you're paranoid, or anything . . .

Size and lung capacity

There are many extraordinary designs in this book, and by the time you reach the end you may have your own bigger and better ideas. However, bear in mind that a bong, pipe, or hookah should not be so long that you cannot reach the bowl to fire it (unless you have a friend to do that for you). Also, the chamber should only contain as much smoke as your lungs can hold in one deep breath (hookahs excluded); otherwise it's a waste.

The Dragon (see page 94) is a mighty fine bong but you will need an extraordinary lung capacity (and probably the lungs of a couple of willing buddies) to exploit it fully.

SAFETY FIRST

Although bong building is a fun way to spend a weekend with your buddies, it should always be conducted with caution—and certainly never attempted while stoned. I know I sound like your dad, but knives, drills, saws, and other hardware tools are potentially dangerous items. A workshop vise should be used for certain projects to ensure that the material being drilled or cut does not slip. Bongologists should wear heavy-duty gloves and a visor for added protection. You have been warned.

Maintaining Your Equipment

As is the case with any cherished item in your possession, your smoking tool should be regularly "serviced" to keep it clean and in good working order. Ideally after each session, disassemble your bong for cleaning. First dispose of the pipe screen (see page 20) and then rinse out the residue sludge from the bowl and stem. Then, using a heavy-duty kitchen sponge and cleaning fluid (see "Cleaning tools," right), scrub the inside of the bong to remove the more stubborn stains. (You might need to use a bottle brush to reach the more inaccessible areas.) Rinse thoroughly and let dry. Insert a fresh pipe screen prior to further use. (If your bong, pipe, or hookah is made from several parts that can be disassembled, it makes the task of cleaning much easier.)

Scraping

One of the coolest things about smoking buds is that even after your stash is all gone, you can still get high. Scraping bongs and hookahs—try using an awl from a pocket knife—not only salvages resin for another hit but is also a necessary part of bong maintenance.

CLEANING TOOLS

Most head shops sell stiff brushes and solution made specifically for cleaning pipes and bongs. If you are willing to spare it, alcohol, particularly vodka, makes a very good bong-cleaning agent, too.

Bong Cleaner

chapter 2

EASY TOKIN'

"So I built myself a bong out of beaker tubes
Then I smoked all them bitches like I'm Pikach

MC Chris, "Bad(dd)Runner"

Congratulations. Now that you're fully apprised of bong basics, it's time to start building. The projects here are pretty straightforward to make and utilize common household items, but they form an ideal foundation to build upon later. Remember, from little hemp seeds do great bongologists grow.

Foil Pipe

"The subtle smoke"

Hit Power:

Freaky Factor:

Smoothness:

Buildin' Time:
2 minutes

This pipe is not only incredibly easy to make but also discreet and small enough to fold away in your wallet. And, once created, it can be reused many times. All you need is some aluminum cooking foil and a pen. A great pipe for use when you are on the move, when time's precious and you need a hit.

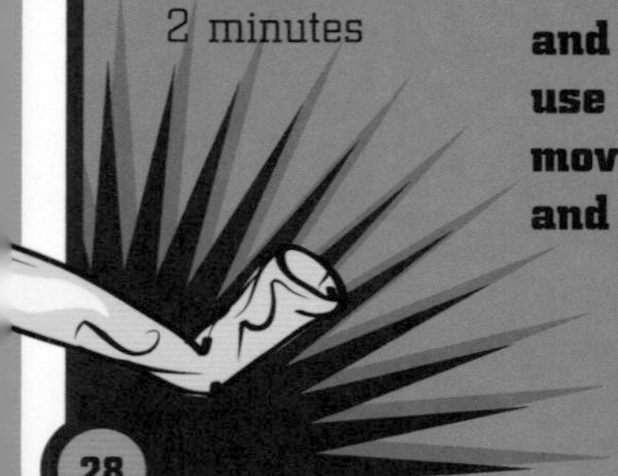

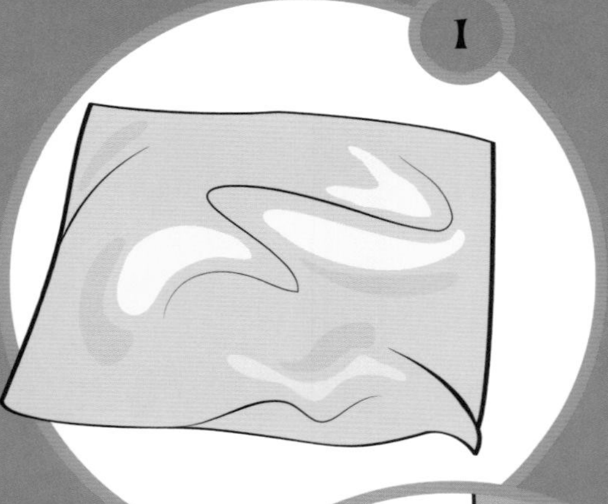

1 First tear off a square of **aluminum foil** measuring about 6 by 6 inches (15 by 15 cm).

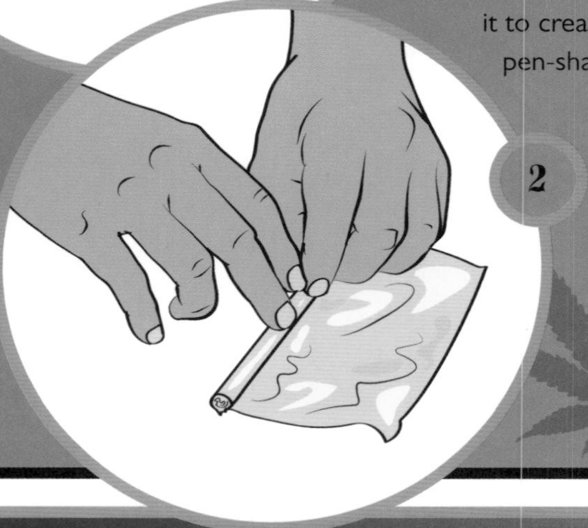

2 Then take a standard cheap **ballpoint pen** and roll the foil around it to create a narrow pen-shaped tube.

3 Now slowly withdraw the pen and just before the end use it to form an upturn in the foil. This is where your weed will sit. Put the pen to one side, its job done.

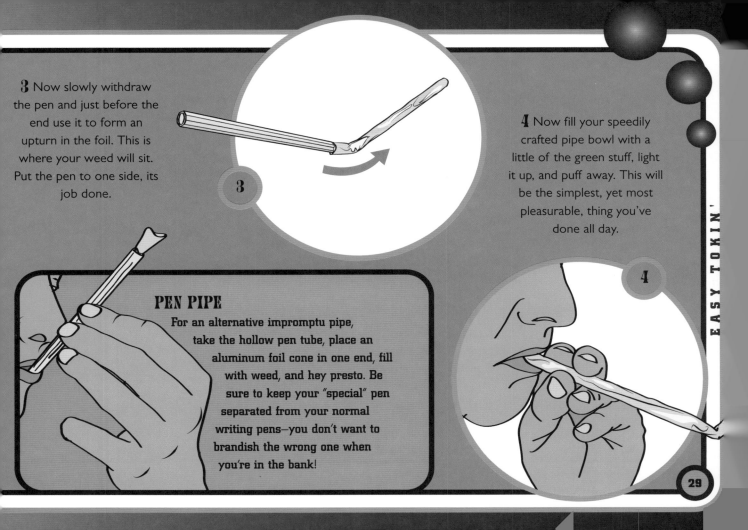

3

4 Now fill your speedily crafted pipe bowl with a little of the green stuff, light it up, and puff away. This will be the simplest, yet most pleasurable, thing you've done all day.

4

PEN PIPE

For an alternative impromptu pipe, take the hollow pen tube, place an aluminum foil cone in one end, fill with weed, and hey presto. Be sure to keep your "special" pen separated from your normal writing pens—you don't want to brandish the wrong one when you're in the bank!

Matchbox Pipe

"Three strikes and you're out"

Hit Power:
🍁🍁🍁🍁🍁

Freaky Factor:
🍁🍁🍁🍁🍁

Smoothness:
🍁🍁🍁🍁🍁

Buildin' Time:
3 minutes

All stoners need a box of matches to light their Js, but when the box is empty it doesn't have to be the end of your fun. With a few minor modifications, that matchbox makes for a great (and unassuming) pipe. Of course, your parents always told you never to play with matches, but they never said anything about matchboxes, so technically this should be perfectly acceptable. Enjoy.

I Take an **empty box of matches**—the box for larger matches, meant for cooking, works best, but a small box works well, too. First, make a hole with a 1/2-inch (12 mm) diameter at one end of the long striking strip, for the bowl, as shown. You can use a **craft knife**, although the pointed end of a **pen** or **pencil** will work just as well.

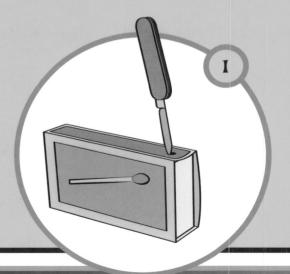

I

3 Finally, add a store-bought or improvised **bowl**, fill it with weed, seal with **putty** if necessary, light it up, and inhale. That's three easy steps to a simple high.

2 Now, open out the drawer at the opposite end and make a similar-sized hole here to act as the mouthpiece.

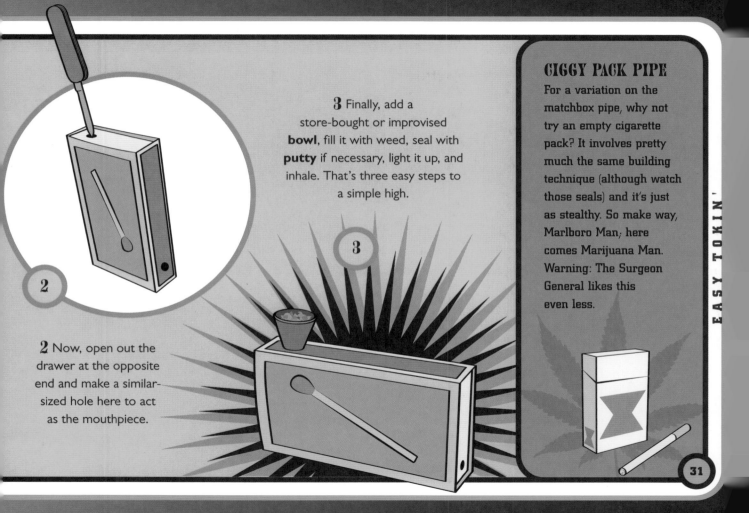

CIGGY PACK PIPE

For a variation on the matchbox pipe, why not try an empty cigarette pack? It involves pretty much the same building technique (although watch those seals) and it's just as stealthy. So make way, Marlboro Man; here comes Marijuana Man. Warning: The Surgeon General likes this even less.

Earth Pipe

"As nature intended"

Hit Power:
🍁🍁🍁🍁🍁

Freaky Factor:
🍁🍁🍁🍁🍁

Smoothness:
🍁🍁🍁🍁🍁

Buildin' Time:
10 minutes

This pipe not only offers a way to feel affinity with the African stoners of a thousand years ago but is also a great way to smoke when you're on a camping trip or at an outdoor music festival—or just feel like getting in touch with Mother Nature. The Earth Pipe requires almost no equipment save for a couple of hollow tubes and your trusty stash. Plus the earthworms get a free hit.

I This simple pipe requires just **two hollow tubes**, an improvised **bowl**, and your not-so-secret ingredient, of course. Any stiff tubes will do, but in keeping with the earth theme, **bamboo** is best. Cut one piece to about 10 inches (25 cm); this will be the mouthpiece. Cut the other to about 6 inches (15 cm); this will be the bowl stem.

2 Bamboo contains various knots and may not be entirely hollow. So, remove any obstructions from the inside with a **kebab skewer** or similar.

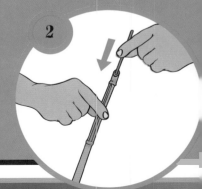

PIPE ANGLE

When cutting your bamboo, trim the ends at a 45-degree angle. This will make the pipes easier to push into the ground, and it will make for a more level receptacle into which the bowl is sealed.

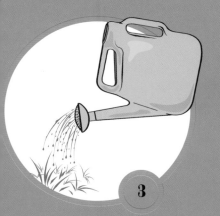

4 Position your bamboo stems about 8 inches apart and push them into the ground at a 45-degree angle. Initially, push them in to their fullest extent so that the tunnels they create are connected; the smoke must be able to flow from one side to the other. Then withdraw the bamboo stems, clean away any mud from the inside of each stem, and reinsert so that approximately half the length of each is below ground.

3 Now choose a patch of earth on which to build your pipe. If the ground is not damp, water the area thoroughly and let it sink in. Damp ground is essential for cooling the smoke as it passes through.

5 Add an herb-filled bowl to the end of the shorter stem and make it airtight by sealing it with **putty**. Then lie on your belly next to the mouthpiece and spark that mother up. Communing with nature has never been such fun.

Apple Bong
"Fruity loopy"

Hit Power:
✳ ✳ ✳ ✳ ✳

Freaky Factor:
✳ ✳ ✳ ✳

Smoothness:
✳ ✳ ✳ ✳ ✳

Buildin' Time:
5 minutes

A hippie classic, the apple bong is a smooth, sweet-tasting smoke, and it's full of vitamin C too. Charlize Theron was famously photographed smoking one of these beauties on a beach in Thailand. And if it's good enough for a Hollywood A-lister, then it's good enough for you. Remember, an apple a day keeps the doctor away.

I Take a ripe and juicy **apple**. With the plastic casing of a **ballpoint pen** (take the ink tube out first), pierce the top of the apple near the stem and create a tunnel through to its core. (You can also use a **potato peeler** or a small **kitchen knife**.)

2

3 Push a **brass bowl** into the first hole, or fashion a bowl out of **aluminum foil** and pierce it with a pin. Add your weed to the bowl, push the plastic pen tube (the mouthpiece) into the second hole, and juice away.

3

2 Then repeat the process on the side of the apple, about 90 degrees to the original hole. Again push the tube through to the middle of the fruit, so that both holes meet up—this is the chamber through which the smoke passes.

SMOKING STRAWBERRIES

Most soft-centered fruit, large or small, is suitable fodder for bongologists. On its smallest scale, a strawberry smoked through two hollow lollipop sticks or narrow straws constitutes a great morning pick-me-up.

Fruity Toot

"Get juiced"

Hit Power:
🌿 🌿 🌿 🌿

Freaky Factor:
🌿 🌿 🌿 🌿

Smoothness:
🌿 🌿 🌿 🌿

Buildin' Time:
5 minutes

Based on a principle similar to that of the classic can pipe, this neat smoking contraption—for years a favorite of South African stoners—can be built and smoked as a pipe or bong. The built-in drinking-straw hole on the top of the juice box saves you from having to make a mouthpiece, too.

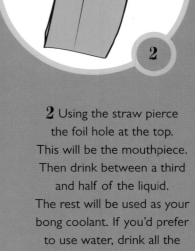

2

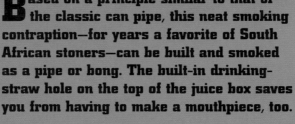

I You will need a **standard juice box**, about 6.75 ounces (¹/3 pint), preferably with a **detachable straw**. Remove the straw.

2 Using the straw pierce the foil hole at the top. This will be the mouthpiece. Then drink between a third and half of the liquid. The rest will be used as your bong coolant. If you'd prefer to use water, drink all the juice in the carton and refill it from the faucet later.

I

3 Now for the bowl. Using a small **craft knife**, make another hole, with a diameter greater than that of the mouthpiece, on the opposite side of the top of the carton, as shown.

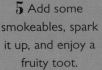

4 Insert a **bowl** purchased from a head shop or made at home, and add some **putty** to make it airtight. A carb hole is optional.

5 Add some smokeables, spark it up, and enjoy a fruity toot.

CAN PIPE

A common alternative to the Fruity Toot involves making two holes in an empty aluminum soda or beer can. However, because the can is used empty, the bongologist doesn't have the benefit of inhaling cooled smoke. And burning weed directly off a hole in an aluminum can will pollute your lungs far more than is desirable, due to the toxic substances produced. Take my advice and stick to the Fruity Toot.

Shotty Bottle

"The original and the best"

Hit Power:
🍁🍁🍁🍁🍁

Freaky Factor:
🍁🍁🍁🍁🍁

Smoothness:
🍁🍁🍁🍁🍁

Buildin' Time:
15 minutes

The art of drawing cannabis smoke through cooling water and into your lungs needn't be complicated. Like all great inventions, the Shotty Bottle is simple, and it's also legendary. In fact, in most smoking circles around the world, the Shotty is the first device any novice bongologist encounters on the long road to greatness. It's made like this:

I

I For this bong, it's best to use a 16.9-ounce (500 ml) plastic water or juice **bottle**, although in truth a beverage bottle of any size will do. First, drill a round hole in the lid that is equal in diameter to that of the plastic casing of a standard ballpoint pen.

2 Next, make a hole of the same size in the neck of the bottle.

2

3 Now remove the lid and fill the bottle half full of water.

4 Take **two ballpoint pens**, and remove and discard the ink tubes and end caps, so you are left with the hollow plastic casings only.

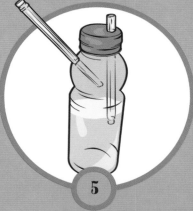

5 Push each of the pen casings into one of the two holes but to different depths—the end of the one in the lid (the bowl) must extend below the water line, and end of the other (the mouthpiece) must be above it. Make the seals airtight.

6 Improvise a bowl from **aluminum foil** (or use **putty** to seal in place a manufactured bowl piece), add some weed, and you're ready for action.

The Lung

"Suck it and see"

Hit Power:
※ ※ ※ ※ ※

Freaky Factor:
※ ※ ※ ※

Smoothness:
※ ※ ※ ※ ※

Buildin' Time:
20 minutes

The first of several designs in this book to use air suction to draw the smoke from the bowl to the chamber, The Lung requires little more than a plastic bottle and an airtight plastic bag. Don't partake from this contraption too often, though, or else you might end up requiring an iron lung to go with it.

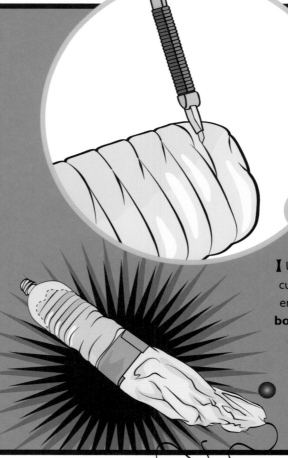

I

I Using a **craft knife**, cut away the bottom end of a 1- or 2-liter **bottle** (approximately 32 or 64 ounces).

2 Get a small- to medium-sized airtight **plastic bag** (a garbage can liner is ideal). Using **duct tape**, seal the open end of the bag around the outside of the bottom of the bottle. Blow through the top of the bottle to check for a tight seal.

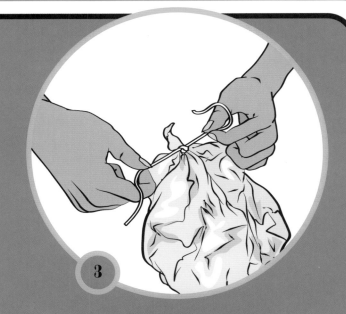

3 Pull the bag out to its fullest length and tie a piece of **string** around a small portion of its end. Once done, tie a loop in the string that's wide enough to fit your foot through.

4 Using your fist, stuff the bag inside the bottle up to the neck. Make sure that the string hangs freely.

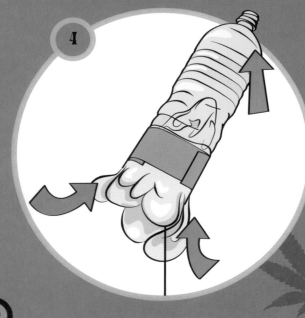

5 Using a **drill**, make a hole in the screw cap to accommodate a **bowl**. Seal around the edge with **putty** if necessary and add some weed to the bowl.

6 Put the string around your foot, hold the bottle at the top with one hand and with your free hand light the bowl. Slowly bring the bottle up so the bag unfolds. As it does so, suction will draw the smoke into the chamber.

7 When the bag is fully extended and the chamber is full of smoke, detach the cap, remove your foot from the string loop, and rapidly suck in the smoke. Then sit down—for at least a half hour.

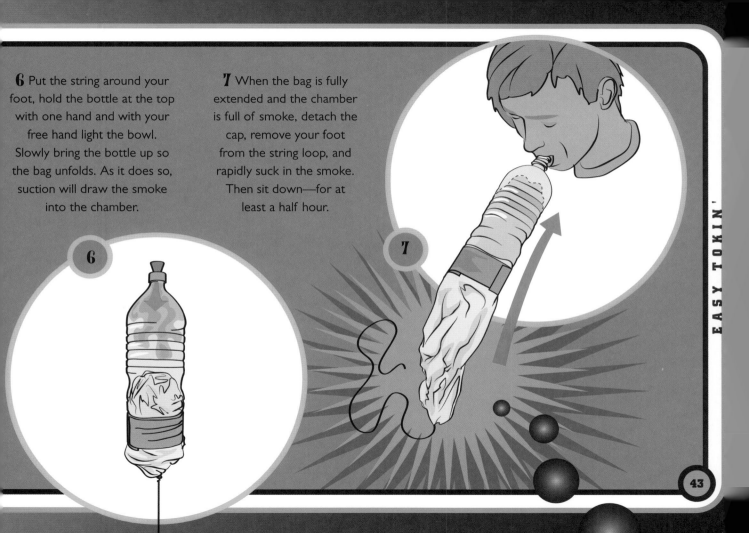

Gravity Bong
"Floatin' feeling"

Hit Power:
🌿🌿🌿🌿🌿

Freaky Factor:
🌿🌿🌿🌿🌿

Smoothness:
🌿🌿🌿🌿

Buildin' Time:
10 minutes

Also known as "The Waterfall," this ingenious device—again utilizing the bongologist-friendly plastic bottle—harnesses the suction power of falling water to draw smoke into the chamber. A few minutes after ingesting a full Gravity Bong you will indeed feel weightless, and fairly mindless. In fact, the head rush is probably somewhat akin to hurling yourself off the top of Niagara Falls. Proceed with caution.

1 It's time for another empty beverage bottle. You should get an award from Greenpeace for this level of recycling. This time, make a small hole in a 1- or 2-liter plastic **bottle** (approximately 32 or 64 ounces), about 1 inch (2.5 cm) up from the bottom. You can do this with a knife, but a lit cigarette with a big cherry works best.

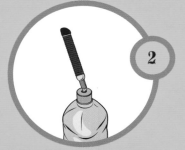

2 Now, using a **craft knife**, make a hole in the cap, large enough to accommodate a **bowl**.

3 Push the bowl in place and make it airtight.

4 Now for the water part of the "waterfall." You may need a friend to help you out with the next couple of steps. Remove the cap and, with your finger covering the hole, fill the bottle to the top with water.

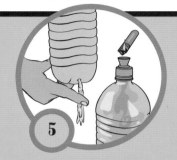

6 When the last of the water has drained away, put your finger back over the hole, unscrew the cap . . .

5 With the hole still plugged, reapply the cap, fill the bowl with smokeables and light it, while at the same time removing your finger from the hole. The smoke will be drawn through the bottom of the bowl and into the bottle chamber via the suction caused by the escaping water.

7 . . . remove your finger, breathe in, and hold. Then watch gravity take hold again, this time on your legs as you slump onto the couch. Sweet dreams.

SPECIAL STOPPER

If you're getting a taste for bongology now and starting to take pride in your work, why not buy (or make) a rubber stopper to go in the hole and save your plump digit all that hard work?

Office Bong

"Work sucks"

Hit Power:
✹ ✹ ✹ ✹ ✹

Freaky Factor:
✹ ✹ ✹ ✹ ✹

Smoothness:
✹ ✹ ✹ ✹ ✹

Buildin' Time:
15 minutes

If you're unfortunate enough to have an uncool "career" working for The Man, you'll probably agree that the morning coffee is the highlight of the day. But the caffeine rush doesn't cut it, despite the fact that your latte costs you $4 (£2.90). To get more for your dollar, why not recycle your cardboard coffee cup into a discreet bong? Trust me, the combination of a double espresso followed by a swift toot will provide a buzz to get you through until five o'clock. Just don't schedule any meetings that day.

I Once you've had your daily caffeine hit, remove the lid, rinse the empty **cup** and fill at least half full with water. Then replace the lid and seal in place with some **tape** from your desk drawer.

2 Now for lid modifications. The lid already features one hole, of course, although this may require enlarging with a **knife** or pair of **scissors** to fit the tubes (see step 3). Make a fresh hole on the opposite edge of the lid, or simply enlarge the pin-prick sized holes that are a feature of some.

3

4 Now take a trip to the office kitchen, supposedly to make yourself another cup of coffee, but actually to get some **aluminum foil**. Returning to your desk, roll a small strip of the foil around the second pen to create a cone-shaped bowl.

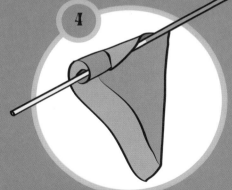

4

3 Next, find a couple of cheap **ballpoint pens**, and remove the ink tubes so you're left with the hollow plastic casings. Insert one into the new hole, but not too far— the bottom end must be above the water level.

5

5 Insert this bowl into one end of the pen and push the other end through the hole in the coffee cup lid—this time ensuring that the bottom end is comfortably below the water level. Finally, add a little cheeky something to the bowl. Without further ado, recline in your swivel chair, set your phone to voice mail, and spark this beauty up as your boss looks on, openmouthed.

Jam-Jar Hookah

"Sweet treat"

Hit Power:
🌿🌿🌿🌿🌿

Freaky Factor:
🌿🌿🌿🌿🌿

Smoothness:
🌿🌿🌿🌿🌿

Buildin' Time:
15 minutes

This simple, one-person hookah is a real delight, and it's easy to make. Glass cannot be drilled (however much of a good idea that might seem to you when you're happily high), so the bowl and mouthpiece operate through the lid. However, it's transparent and you can see the weed smoke as it fills the chamber. Nice.

I Take a standard empty jam or mayonnaise **jar**, wash it thoroughly, and allow it to dry. Making sure that the lid is screwed on firmly, use an **awl** and a **hammer** to make two pilot holes in the lid as shown.

2 Then secure the jar in a **vise** and bore holes through the lid with a **drill**.

4 Insert the downpipe into the hole so it is below the water level. Secure the bowl in place with a **rubber washer** and add a **putty seal** if required.

5 Remove the lid and fill the jar about half full either with water or a fruit-based juice like raspberry or strawberry.

6 Insert the mouthpiece (it must be above the water line) and seal. Then load the bowl and prepare for your day to go up in smoke, literally.

3 Now it's time for the bowl and mouthpiece. First screw a bong **bowl** into a **downpipe** that is almost as deep as the jar—approximately 4 to 5 inches (10 to 12 cm), or fashion your own from a copper heating pipe. Also cut a piece of **vinyl hose** to a similar length—this will be the mouthpiece.

chapter **3**

TAKE A
FRESH HIT

"Load up the bong, crank up the song
Let the informa call 911"

Sublime, "Get Ready"

Now it's time to up your game and start mixing with the big boys. From the sublime (Party Hookah) to the ridiculous (Teapot Bong and The Mask)—by way of hardware-store staples like Drain Pipe and Ballcock Bong—there are enough projects in this chapter to fill your weekends for the next month.

Party Hookah

"Celebrate, and have a good time"

Hit Power:
✹ ✹ ✹ ✹

Freaky Factor:
✹ ✹ ✹ ✹

Smoothness:
✹ ✹ ✹ ✹

Buildin' Time:
20 minutes

The time must come in the tuition of all bongologists when they strike out and "go large." And the Party Hookah is just that opportunity. Trust me, if you're holding a birthday get-together, nothing will attract your guests like the promise of a blast on this monster. Of course, the next day, you won't remember anything about the evening, but that just means you had a good time. Bring on next year.

I A hookah for the masses (well, at least three people) requires a large chamber. You can use a 128-ounce (3.8 L) juice **bottle**, but a 5-gallon (20 L) **water cooler** is better—and frankly more impressive. When it's about two-thirds empty, it's ready for use. The lids on these monsters tend to be pretty much immovable, but no problem. Use a **hammer** and **screwdriver** to pry out the dispensing nozzle.

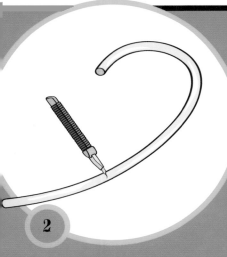

2

2 Next, cut several lengths of flexible **vinyl hose**. The downpipe should be as long as the bottle is deep, about 2 feet (80 cm); the mouthpiece tubes (as many as you want) should be about half that length.

3 Next, you will prepare a **bowl and downpipe combo**. You can make your own from a **brass nozzle** and **copper heating pipe**, buy one from a head shop, or reuse a unit from a store-bought bong. Add a **rubber washer** just below the bowl.

3

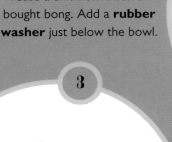

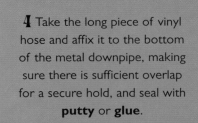

4

4 Take the long piece of vinyl hose and affix it to the bottom of the metal downpipe, making sure there is sufficient overlap for a secure hold, and seal with **putty** or **glue**.

6 Now for the mouthpieces. Make a series of holes with a **craft knife** at an equal height around the perimeter of the cooler about 6 inches (15 cm) down from the bottom of the cap.

5

6

5 Lower this combo, vinyl tube first, into the top of the water cooler. Press the bowl into the washer to guarantee a tight seal.

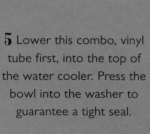

SOLO NO-NO
If, for whatever reason, no one shows up at the party (you probably gave everyone the wrong date, you dumbass), do not seek to raise your spirits by indulging in the Party Hookah alone—it could be the last thing you do for a while.

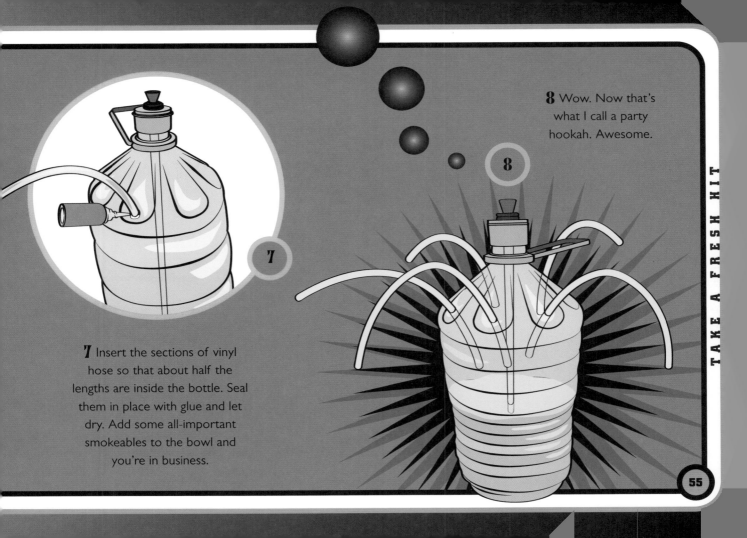

7 Insert the sections of vinyl hose so that about half the lengths are inside the bottle. Seal them in place with glue and let dry. Add some all-important smokeables to the bowl and you're in business.

8 Wow. Now that's what I call a party hookah. Awesome.

The Bucket

"Beyond the pail (sic)"

Hit Power:
🌿🌿🌿🌿🌿

Freaky Factor:
🌿🌿🌿🌿🌿

Smoothness:
🌿🌿🌿🌿🌿

Buildin' Time:
15 minutes

One of the greatest summer party bongs, The Bucket is simple and devastatingly effective. Once the party's in full swing, set up a large bucket of water, grab your modified plastic bottle, load the bowl, and get your guests to form a line. Just don't christen The Bucket too early in the evening (or too frequently), unless a backyard full of gibbering idiots is your idea of a good time.

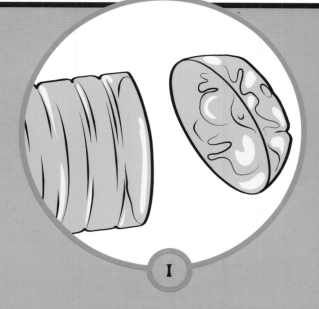

I

I It's once again time for the trusty plastic beverage bottle. Using a **craft knife**, cut away the bottom end of a 2-liter **bottle** (approximately 64 ounces).

2 Now make a hole in the lid of the bottle and affix a **bowl**. Seal it in place with **putty** and screw the cap back onto the bottle.

3 Now fill a clean **bucket** at least half full of water.

4

4 You might need a friend to help you with the next part, especially if you've already had a few smokes. Slowly push the bottle bottom-first into the bucket of water. Stop when the water level on the inside is just below the cap. Then add some weed to the bowl, light it . . .

5 . . . and start to draw the bottle up and out of the water very slowly. As you do so, the water pressure will draw smoke from the burning weed down into the bottle. Stop when the bottle is submerged just an inch or two. Don't cut this too close, since you don't want any smoke to escape.

SOGGY WEED

Don't put the weed in the bowl before you push the bottle into the water. In that event, all you'd do is fire the weed out of the bowl and into the water—and then you'd have to start over.

5

7 . . . and before any smoke escapes place your mouth over the hole. Slowly push your head down into the bucket, forcing the smoke into your lungs. Sweet.

6 Now, using your (ahem) lightning fast reflexes, unscrew the cap . . .

MULTI-BUCKET

If one bucket simply isn't enough to satisfy the voracious appetite of you and your guests, prepare two or more bottles (as above), and then tape the necks securely to a length of wood such as a broom handle. Next, lower them, as one unit, into a bathtub. But be prepared to suffer the consequences of this idiotic act. In the immortal words of Mr. T, "You crazy fools."

6

7

Drain Pipe

"The plumber's favorite"

Hit Power:
🌿 🌿 🌿 🌿 🌿

Freaky Factor:
🌿 🌿 🌿 🌿 🌿

Smoothness:
🌿 🌿 🌿 🌿 🌿

Buildin' Time:
10 minutes

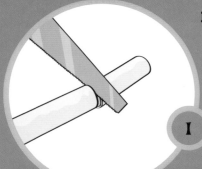

As previously noted, the hardware store is a real treasure trove for bongologists—and no more so than with the materials for this smoking contraption. Head down to the local store, find the plumbing aisle, and all will be revealed. But don't let your boo see you—she might think (heaven forbid) that you're planning some DIY home renovations.

1 Position a length of **plumber's pipe** (of any diameter) on a **workbench**. Using a **saw**, cut a piece of pipe 6 to 8 inches (15 to 20 cm) long with a straight edge.

2 Now, for a change of direction, get a 90-degree-angled **pipe bend**. It's time to send your smoke round corners.

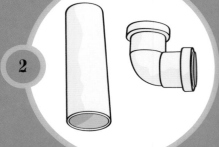

BOLD AS BRASS

The same smoking pipe can be built with brass and copper pipes and bends, the type used for conducting hot water. These will be more expensive, however.

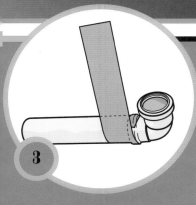

3 Slot the pipe bend into position at one end of the straight pipe and seal it in place with **duct tape**.

4 Now it's time to prepare the bowl end. If your pipe bend has too large a diameter for your bowl, slot a piece of slightly narrower pipe in place first (no more than 2 inches (5 cm) long). Then insert your **bowl**, secure with a **rubber washer**, and use further sealant if required.

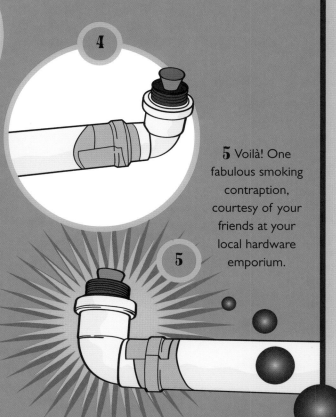

5 Voilà! One fabulous smoking contraption, courtesy of your friends at your local hardware emporium.

SHAPE SHIFTING

Armed with a long length of drain pipe and several 90-degree-angled bend pieces, all of which can be bought for less than $8 to $10 (£5 or so), you can create some contraptions of eye-popping proportions, from the standard S shape to a nearly full circle. But before you get too silly and start building something that tracks around your house, remember that the bowl needs to be within an arm's length for you to light it.

Bellows Bong

"God of Hellfire"

Hit Power:
✿ ✿ ✿ ✿ ✿

Freaky Factor:
✿ ✿ ✿ ✿ ✿

Smoothness:
✿ ✿ ✿ ✿ ✿

Buildin' Time:
5 minutes

I Get an ordinary set of **fire bellows** and prepare for mischief. First, making sure the bellows are fully depressed, add an appropriately sized **rubber washer** to the draw hole in the top. Then push a **bowl** into the washer and seal in place with **putty**.

If you live in an area with a warm climate, the concept of a log fire in the fireplace might be a bit foreign. But if you live in an area with cold winter nights, you no doubt have a set of bellows for starting fires. And what better way to warm up on long nights in your log cabin than with a bellows bong.

2 Sprinkle some of Mary Jane's finest into the bowl . . .

3 . . . and then light the bowl while raising the handles of the bellows to draw in the smoke.

4 When the bellows are full, twist them around, place the nozzle to your lips and slowly depress the handles, ejecting the smoke into your mouth. Then settle back. You'll soon feel as warm and cozy as you would sitting in front of the best log fire ever.

Recorder Pipe

"Musical marijuana"

Hit Power:
🌿🌿🌿🌿🌿

Freaky Factor:
🌿🌿🌿🌿🌿

Smoothness:
🌿🌿🌿🌿🌿

Buildin' Time:
10 minutes

Music and drug use are intrinsically linked; many a famous rock guitarist, bassist, and drummer has dabbled with Mary Jane. But, generally speaking, those who favor wind instruments tend not to be as hedonistic as the Keith Richards types. But that doesn't preclude the recorder from making a perfect pipe. So load up your weed, spark it up, and let your fingers hit the "high" notes.

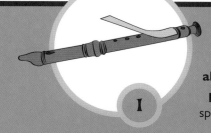

I The first thing you'll notice about this musical instrument is that, although it is perfectly pipe shaped, it features far too many holes to make a suitable smoking device. So, get some **duct tape** and seal all the finger holes apart from the mouthpiece, the end piece (known as the foot joint), and the farthest finger hole, at the far end. Note that there is one additional thumb hole on the underside of the recorder, which also requires sealing.

2 Now, fashion a bowl cone from a small piece of **aluminum foil** (wrap it around a **pen** to get the shape) or use a specially constructed **bowl** from a head shop, and place it in the remaining uncovered finger hole.

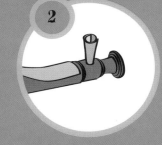

3 Put some weed in and start to "play."

Caribbean Smile

"A tropical delight"

Hit Power:
🌿 🌿 🌿 🌿 🌿

Freaky Factor:
🌿 🌿 🌿 🌿 🌿

Smoothness:
🌿 🌿 🌿

Buildin' Time:
25 minutes

Your two-week vacation is priceless—you've spent all year working for The Man, and you sure don't wanna waste it visiting museums. So head for the beach and put your feet up, with a rum punch in one hand and a Caribbean Smile in the other. Not only will this fruity bong get you mighty stoned, but it's also a step toward your five fruits and vegetables a day!

I First, take **two carrots** (one about 8 inches long and quite slender, the other a little shorter and stubbier).

2 Using a **kebab skewer** or **vegetable corer**, carefully hollow out both carrots.

2

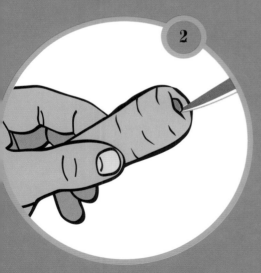

3

3 Then take a **pineapple** and make a large hole (wide enough to accommodate the fat carrot), using a **knife** at a slight angle about halfway through the fruit. Position the fat carrot in this hole.

GOT NO CARROTS?

If you don't have any carrots, don't despair—any plastic or metal tube (such as a pen casing) will do for the bowl and tokin' pipes. Just make your holes a suitable size to fit.

4 Next, using the knife again, create a second hole on the side of the pineapple at about 90 degrees to the first so that the two meet in the center. This is crucial. This will be the tokin' hole. Position the other carrot in this hole.

5 Using the same cutting technique, create a third hole (an inch or so away from the top hole) that will meet up with your existing chamber system. This "carb" can be essentially anywhere on the pineapple, but you'll want it to be convenient enough so you can cover it with a finger while you're lighting your mix.

GETTING FRUITY

Fruit bongs hold your mix nicely, are easily disposed of, and are biodegradable. If you are really hard up you may even want to eat the fruit when finished. Apart from pineapples, apples, squashes, cucumbers, and mango, many other choices will impart their own flavor to your smoke, so you'll never get bored.

6 Next, taking some **aluminum foil**, make a small bowl, big enough to hold the quantity of grass or hash you want to smoke. Make a number of small pin pricks in the bottom of the bowl and fold the edges over the top of the stubby carrot.

7 Finally, load the bowl and bubble away.

Teapot Bong
"A class apart"

Hit Power:
🌿🌿🌿🌿🌿

Freaky Factor:
🌿🌿🌿🌿🌿

Smoothness:
🌿🌿🌿🌿🌿

Buildin' Time:
15 minutes

To the English upper classes the teapot is one of the last great vestiges of the British Empire; it represents civilized living and afternoon tea. To the likes of you and me it represents the chance to make a perfectly disguised bong. Just drill a small hole opposite the spout and you are ready. Make sure it's well hidden when your lady invites the posh relatives over for cucumber sandwiches.

1 Take a common **teapot**. Ceramic or metal is fine, as long as the inside of the spout is positioned at least halfway up. Fill it with water below the level of the spout. (Teapots with spout openings very near the bottom are not suitable as bongs because of the required water level.)

2 The teapot will have a small hole in the lid. It's intended to release excess steam during brewing, but it also makes the life of any bongologist easier. However, for this bong, the hole needs to be bigger. First, mask the hole thoroughly with **duct tape** or similar.

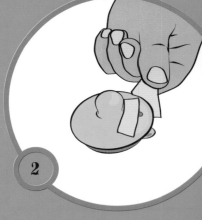

3 Secure the lid firmly in a **vise** and **drill** through.

3

4

4 Cut a length of **vinyl hose** (¹/₈ inch, or 6 mm, in diameter) and about as long as the teapot is deep—4 to 6 inches (10 to 15 cm) should do it. Insert the tube through the hole so only about an inch is visible above the lid.

5 Affix a **bowl and downpipe combo** to the top of the tube and replace the lid on the teapot. Pack the bowl with weed, light it, and suck through the spout.

LIFTING THE LID

You can drill a second, smaller, hole in the lid if you wish to have a carb, but it's just as easy to lift the lid very slightly.

5

Backyard Bong

"Essential tool of the weed farmer"

Hit Power:

Freaky Factor:

Smoothness:

Buildin' Time:
15 minutes

When you're looking around the house for inspiratio certain items just scream, "USE ME." In the kitche the classic candidates are the kettle and teapot (see pa 68). The backyard, however, is the sole domain of the watering can. This is how to misuse one:

I First things first. Fill your **watering can** with some agua. How much depends on the design of your can, but it must be below the bottom of the spout.

2 Next, take a section of **plumbing pipe** with a diameter that is slightly narrower than that of the hole at the top of the can. Lower it into the can until it touches the bottom, then mark a position about 1 inch (2.5 cm) up from the top of the can.

3 Remove the pipe and cut it to that length. If you require a further small length of tubing to better accommodate your bowl (the original pipe may be too wide), cut that to size also.

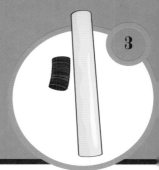

4 Position the pipe or pipes in the can. Then seal them with **duct tape** or a **glue gun** so there are no gaps around the edge.

5 Then insert a **bowl and downpipe** and secure it in place with a **rubber washer**. Add further sealant if required.

6 Mark a position for a small carb hole near the top of the can, and drill the hole.

7 Fill the bowl with your garden's finest crop, place your mouth over the spout and roar away.

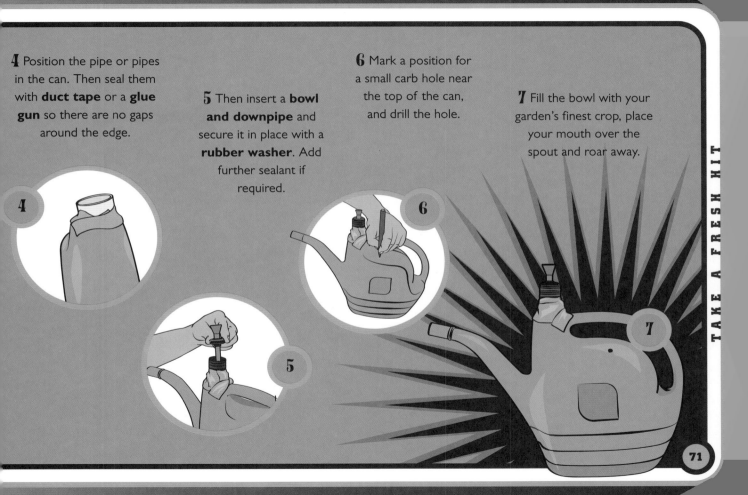

TAKE A FRESH HIT

71

The Compressor

"The chamber of horrors"

Hit Power:
🍁🍁🍁🍁🍁

Freaky Factor:
🍁🍁🍁🍁🍁

Smoothness:
🍁🍁🍁🍁🍁

Buildin' Time:
25 minutes

Are you still conscious? Good, because it's time to crank up your education a little more. For this next project you will need a standard large plastic beverage bottle, and an outlet hose for a vented clothes dryer—probably not something you'd ever considered useful for your tokin' career. But, believe me, the blast from this contraption really hits the spot.

I

I Fully extend a portion of the **hose** to around 2 feet (60 cm) and, using a set of **wire cutters**, snip the metal frame that houses the plastic covering. Now fit the larger section back on your dryer and hope your landlord never notices.

2 The smaller section is destined for better things. But first you need to fashion a top and bottom for your Compressor. Take an empty 2-liter beverage **bottle** (approximately 64 ounces) and make one cut all the way around, about 4 inches (10 cm) down from the neck (as shown) . . .

3

2

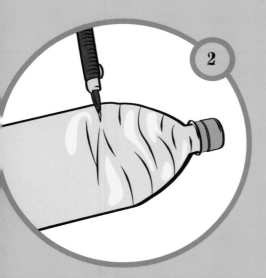

3 . . . and make another cut about 3 inches (7.5 cm) from the bottom. You don't need the middle section, but keep it for another day and another bong.

4 Place the bottom portion of the bottle inside one end of the hose and secure it in place with **duct tape** . . .

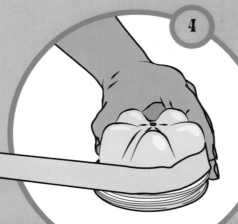

4

5 . . . then repeat the process for the top of the bottle and the other end of the hose. Essentially, you now have an expandable bottle, the dryer hose having taken the place of the bottle's midsection.

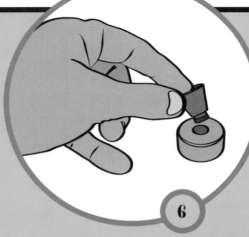

6 Now that the main chamber has been built, turn your attentions to the **bowl**. Make an incision in the bottle cap, and then cut a hole large enough to accommodate a bowl. Insert the bowl and seal if needed, and retighten the cap on the bottle. Now add some smokeables.

7 With the hose fully condensed, light the bowl while drawing the top of the bottle upward.

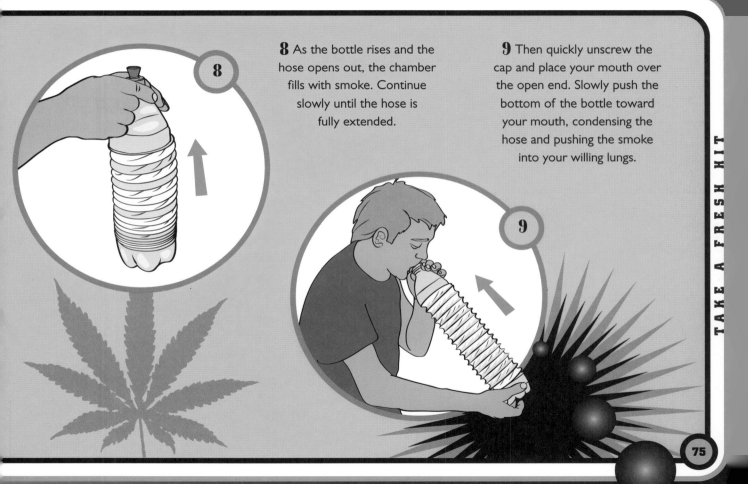

8 As the bottle rises and the hose opens out, the chamber fills with smoke. Continue slowly until the hose is fully extended.

9 Then quickly unscrew the cap and place your mouth over the open end. Slowly push the bottom of the bottle toward your mouth, condensing the hose and pushing the smoke into your willing lungs.

Piggy Bong

"Money madness"

Hit Power:

Freaky Factor:

Smoothness:

Buildin' Time:
10 minutes

If you're a parent you will feel that there is something inherently wrong about stealing your offspring's piggy bank and using it to smoke weed. Yes, it's highly immoral. But the bottom line is that a piggy bank makes a great bong. Besides, after the first hit, any guilt you might feel will soon pass. Be sure to buy little Jonny some ice cream to make good.

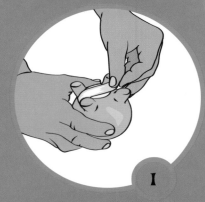

I

I Take a **piggy bank** and prepare to make modifications. If it's in use, first remove all the money and use it to buy some weed. Then put the **plastic stopper** back in place and make it watertight, using **duct tape** or a **glue gun**.

2

2 Next, get some narrow **vinyl tubing** (about 1/8 inch, or 3 mm, in diameter). Use a **craft knife** to cut two lengths, each approximately 6 inches (15 cm) long.

3 Push one of the tubes through one end of the money slot on the top of the pig, so about half the length is inside, and affix a **bowl** with a **rubber washer** at the top.

3

4

4 Now the important part of any bong—the water. Fill the pig through the slot about halfway up so the water level covers the bottom of the tube.

6 Finally, add some weed to the bowl, put your head in the trough and bubble away. Then satiate your munchies with a ham sandwich.

5 Insert the second piece of tubing at the other end of the money slot. This will be the mouthpiece. Make sure that the bottom end of the tube is above the water level.

5

6

SHOT HOLE
Keep your finger covering the gap in the money slot during inhalation. Release to clear the smoke from the chamber.

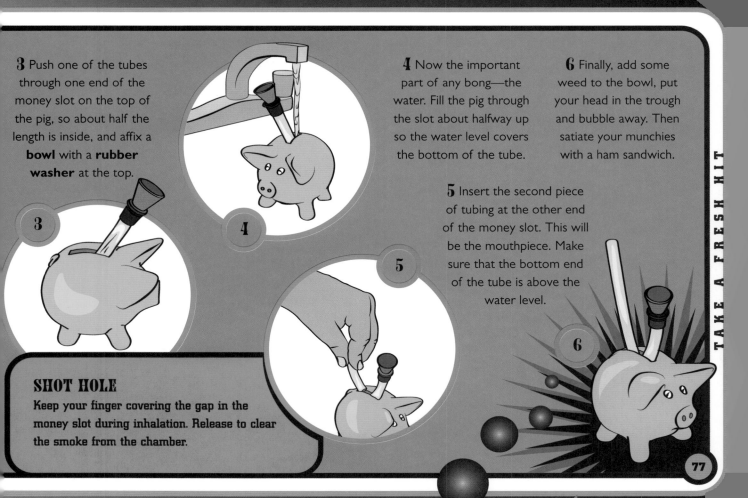

The Mask

"Gas panic!"

Hit Power:
🌿🌿🌿🌿

Freaky Factor:
🌿🌿🌿🌿

Smoothness:
🌿🌿🌿🌿🌿

Buildin' Time:
15 minutes

We've all got one of those elderly relatives who drone on endlessly about "the war." But next Thanksgiving, when your uncle starts to recall his tour of duty in 'Nam for the ninety-fourth time, don't immediately leave the room and roll a fatty. Indulge him a little and ask if he still owns his gas mask—it could be the most rewarding conversation you've ever had.

1

I First take your **gas mask** and match the diameter of the inhaling nozzle with a piece of **corrugated plastic tubing** from the hardware store. Cut a length of the tubing to between 12 and 18 inches (30 to 46 cm).

2 Then cut a matching diameter hole in the nozzle of the mask using a **craft knife**.

2

3 Next, insert a **bowl and downpipe combo** into one end of the plastic tube and secure it in place with a **rubber washer**. Seal with **duct tape** or a **glue gun** if required.

4 Now, insert the free end of the tube into the inhalation nozzle and seal with a glue gun. Allow to dry.

5 Finally, place the mask securely over your face and put your stash box in your pocket. Then retreat to your bunker and await Armageddon.

4

3

5

BONGOLOGY

Ballcock Bong

"Keep on rolling"

Hit Power:
🌿🌿🌿🌿🌿

Freaky Factor:
🌿🌿🌿🌿🌿

Smoothness:
🌿🌿🌿🌿🌿

Buildin' Time:
20 minutes

1 Take a **pen** and mark your ballcock (also called a "balltap" or "fill valve") in three places around its perimeter about a third of the w_ from the top, where the hole for the cistern arm already exists. Two should be on opposite sides (the dual mouthpieces) and one should b_ an equal distance between the other two (this will be the carb).

2 Drill three holes. The two mouthpieces should be wide enough to accommodate a piece of **vinyl hose** about 1/4 inch (60 mm) in diameter. The carb hole should be narrower.

Another hardware store favorite, the Ballcock Bong is a winner on several levels. It costs less than a dollar, it's watertight, it already comes with a hole for your downpipe and bowl combo, it's a dual smoke, and it's quick and easy to make. So what are you still doing here? Get out and build one now.

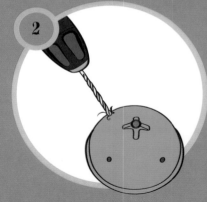

KEEP SMILING
Pimp your ballcock by painting it yellow and adding a black smiley face.

5 Insert a **bowl and downpipe** into the cistern arm hole. Make sure that the end of the downpipe is comfortably below the water level. Secure with a **rubber washer** and seal if necessary.

4 Cut two lengths of **vinyl tubing**, approximately 8 inches (20 cm) long, with a **craft knife**.

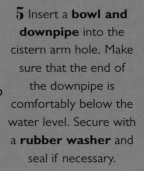

6 Add your two mouthpiece tubes, checking to make sure that they are above the water level, and seal with **putty**. Then spark it up and share a few hits with a significant other.

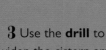

3 Use the **drill** to widen the cistern arm hole if necessary. Fill your ballcock about half full of water.

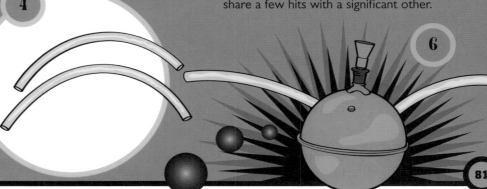

chapter

4

PRO PUFFER

"Sing my song, puff all night long
As I take hits from the bong . . ."

Cypress Hill, "Hits from the Bong"

Congratulations, you've come a long way since you made the Foil Pipe. This is where the challenge gets really interesting. In this section you will find double chambers, triple bowls, and even an electric-powered bong. So take a deep breath (if your lungs still allow) and prepare to reach the zenith of your art.

Fully Loaded

"Shoot 'em up"

Hit Power:
✹✹✹✹✹

Freaky Factor:
✹✹✹✹✹

Smoothness:
✹✹✹✹✹

Buildin' Time:
25 minutes

If you're like me, you've probably still got a box full of toy guns from your childhood stored in your attic—maybe it's being taught the Second Amendment in high school that makes it so we can't bear to throw them away. If you don't have one, buy one at a garage sale. Toy guns make great, discreet pipes. But don't be tempted to use it outdoors—you'd be arrested on two offenses.

I Take a **toy gun**. Remove the screws and strip out any wires or other working contents from the insides so you are left with the outer shell. Keep the trigger for aesthetics, however.

2 Cut a piece of **clear vinyl tube** that is about 3 inches (7.5 cm) longer than the length of the gun. Pushing first through the end of the muzzle, feed it back through the barrel and out the back of the gun below the hammer. Leave a short section of about 3 inches protruding from the back end; this is the mouthpiece. For now at least, leave about an inch overlapping the muzzle.

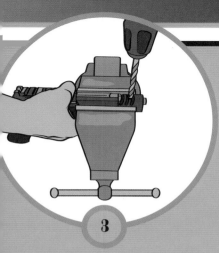

3

4 When you are satisfied with both holes, take the gun apart once more. Now insert a bong **bowl**, or make your own, into the hole in the vinyl tube. Then rebuild the gun for the final time and snip off the spare hose at the end of the muzzle.

4

OUTTA SIGHT

If your toy gun comes with a detachable sight, use it to get a magnified perspective when firing up the bowl.

3 Now you need to create a hole in the gun shell and vinyl tube about an inch from the end of the muzzle. This requires a steady hand and the deployment of two techniques: first, reassemble the gun and use a **drill** to bore into the nozzle; then disassemble the gun and use a **craft knife** to cut into the exposed tube directly below this hole. Do not cut all the way through the tube.

5 Finally, load some "bullets" and prepare to take the ultimate hit from your "woozy" 9 mm.

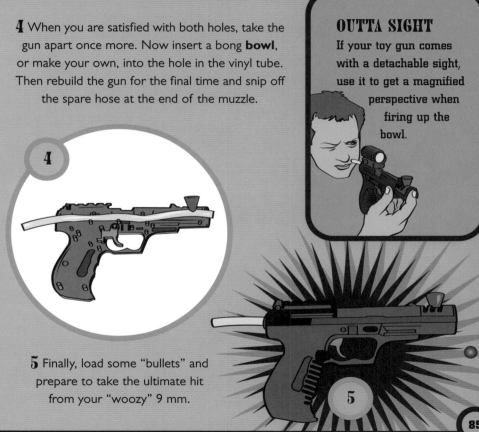

5

Triple X

"The multi-bowled hookah"

Hit Power:
🍁🍁🍁🍁🍁

Freaky Factor:
🍁🍁🍁🍁🍁

Smoothness:
🍁🍁🍁🍁🍁

Buildin' Time:
15 minutes

1 Make three equally spaced holes just below the neck of an empty 2-liter beverage **bottle** (about 64 ounces). These will be the holes for three mouthpieces.

2 Next, cut a short length of **plastic plumbing tube**, about 4 inches (10 cm) long. Then connect three **bowl and pipe combos** and affix a **rubber washer** to each.

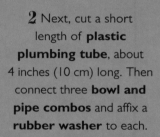

Is one loaded bowl simply not enough for ya? Then don't restrict yourself. Again using a plastic beverage bottle (the bongologist's trusty friend) as the main chamber, fashion a trio of bowls. If you're Tommy Chong, then one mouthpiece may be sufficient, but if you're a lesser mortal, add another two and get a couple of buddies to help you out.

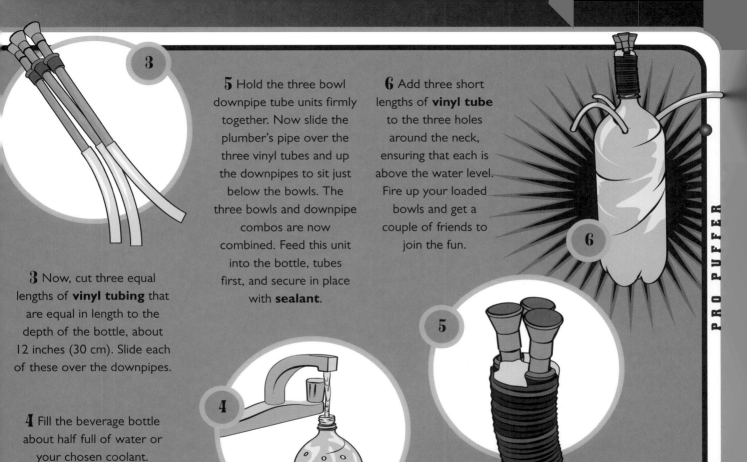

3

3 Now, cut three equal lengths of **vinyl tubing** that are equal in length to the depth of the bottle, about 12 inches (30 cm). Slide each of these over the downpipes.

4 Fill the beverage bottle about half full of water or your chosen coolant.

5 Hold the three bowl downpipe tube units firmly together. Now slide the plumber's pipe over the three vinyl tubes and up the downpipes to sit just below the bowls. The three bowls and downpipe combos are now combined. Feed this unit into the bottle, tubes first, and secure in place with **sealant**.

6 Add three short lengths of **vinyl tube** to the three holes around the neck, ensuring that each is above the water level. Fire up your loaded bowls and get a couple of friends to join the fun.

4

5

6

PRO PUFFER

Keg of Dread

"There's trouble brewing"

Hit Power:
🌿 🌿 🌿 🌿 🌿

Freaky Factor:
🌿 🌿 🌿 🌿 🌿

Smoothness:
🌿 🌿 🌿 🌿 🌿

Buildin' Time:
30 minutes

As anyone who has ever overindulged simultaneously with both substances will acknowledge, weed and beer don't mix. However, that isn't always the case. A small beer keg, emptied of the demon drink, does make for an excellent bong or hookah. Every college student should own one.

I First, drain your **keg** of beer—but not all at once, obviously. Invite your buddies over for a smoke-free evening to finish it off. Next day, using a **hammer** and an **awl** or **screwdriver**, bang through the hose-connector hole at the top.

2 Secure the keg between two very heavy objects and **drill** a 1/4-inch hole at any point near the edge of the keg top. This will serve as the suction pipe hole.

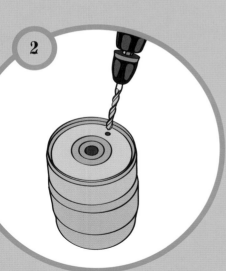

3 Now cut a length of **vinyl hose** about 10 inches (25 cm) long, insert it into the mouthpiece hole, and seal it with **putty** or a **glue gun**.

4 Your hookah is taking shape. Now take it to a faucet and fill it about half full of water or your chosen coolant.

5 Next, you'll make the bowl unit. First, measure the depth of the beer keg, then cut a section of the vinyl hose that is almost that length.

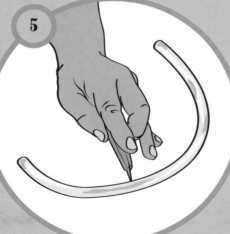

6 Pick up your head-shop **downpipe** (or your own, created from copper heating pipe), add **rubber seals**, and affix the vinyl hose to the bottom end. Make sure there is enough overlap for a secure hold, and seal if necessary.

ANY EMPTIES?

For ease of emptying your hookah, open the tap at the foot of the keg that is designed for pouring the beer. In order to refill it with fresh water you will have to break the seal around the bowl, however.

7 Lower the unit (hose first) into the main hole at the top. Thread a **bowl** piece onto the downpipe and ensure all seals are airtight.

8 Your completed beer keg hookah is now ripe for abuse.

The Cone

"Road trippin'"

Hit Power:
🌿🌿🌿🌿

Freaky Factor:
🌿🌿🌿🌿

Smoothness:
🌿🌿🌿🌿

Buildin' Time:
40 minutes

Invented in 1914 by Charles P. Rudabaker, the humble traffic cone led a prosaic existence on the world's highways until it became the headgear of choice for drunken students everywhere. Now a firm favorite of the stoner community, it is the perfect tool to misuse due to its large size, bulbous shape, and luminous color. One shudders to think what Rudabaker would have made of all this . . .

I Take an ordinary **traffic cone** (of the size to suit your smoking appetite and the number of buddies you want to share it with). Remove the weighted black stand and discard.

2 The wider end of the cone needs to fit snugly into a large receptacle— a **builder's bucket** is ideal. The cone will probably need to be trimmed for the purpose, so rest the cone on a **workbench** and, using a **saw**, cut it to size.

3 Push the cone into the bucket. Seal it in place with a **glue gun** and leave it to dry. Your behemoth bong is starting to take shape.

5 Next, take a roll of **vinyl hose** (1/8 inch, or 3 mm, in diameter) and measure it out from the tip of the cone to the bottom of the bucket. Cut it to size using a **craft knife**.

4 Now fill your newly fused bucket-and-cone combo about half full of water through the hole in the top of the cone.

THE DRAGON

Essentially the big and very bad brother of The Bucket, The Dragon uses a traffic cone instead of a plastic beverage bottle; a roll-out trash container takes the place of the bucket. Only those with obscenely large lung capacities need apply, because not even St. George could slay this monster.

6 Fit a large **rubber washer** to a **bowl and downpipe combo**. This needs to fit snugly into the hole at the top of the cone. Affix the length of vinyl hose to the bottom of the downpipe and set it in position inside the cone.

7 Now for the mouthpiece. Mark a point around the circumference of the cone, about 6 to 8 inches (15 to 20 cm) from the top. Make a 1/8-inch-diameter hole using a **drill** or **craft knife**.

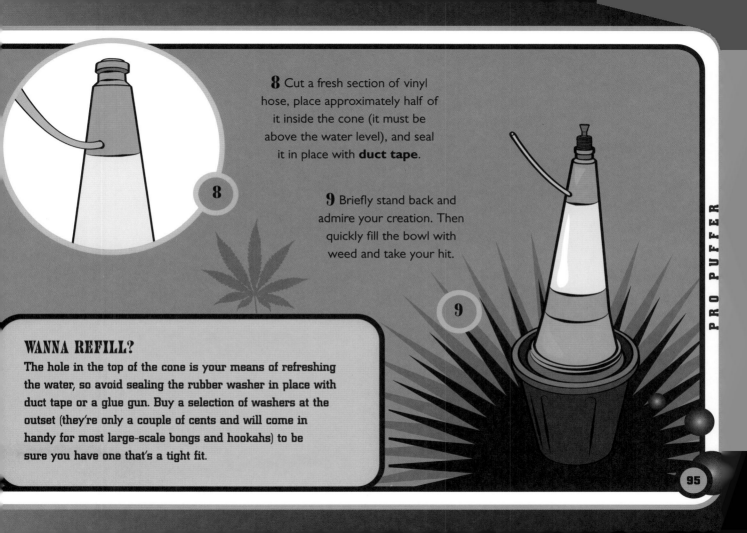

8 Cut a fresh section of vinyl hose, place approximately half of it inside the cone (it must be above the water level), and seal it in place with **duct tape**.

9 Briefly stand back and admire your creation. Then quickly fill the bowl with weed and take your hit.

WANNA REFILL?

The hole in the top of the cone is your means of refreshing the water, so avoid sealing the rubber washer in place with duct tape or a glue gun. Buy a selection of washers at the outset (they're only a couple of cents and will come in handy for most large-scale bongs and hookahs) to be sure you have one that's a tight fit.

Roulette

"The six-shooter"

Hit Power:
🍁🍁🍁🍁

Freaky Factor:
🍁🍁🍁🍁

Smoothness:
🍁🍁🍁🍁

Buildin' Time:
1 to 2 hours

As any gambler knows, roulette is a game of chance. The Roulette pipe is one of the more complicated projects any bongologist can attempt, but the payoff is well worth it. Load the bowls, spin the barrel, and take what's coming to you. Will you get a nice, clean hit or will you get a bowl of mind-blowing weed that your buddy loaded up? Only time will tell.

I

I As the name implies, for a six-shooter you need six bowls. Use 45-degree **angled bowls**, which are readily available at all good head shops. Alternatively, if you're handy with a tool kit, you can fashion your own from **copper pipes** and **brass nozzles**.

2 Now you need two pieces of **acrylic tubing**. One of these, black in this example, needs to be about 8 to 12 inches (20 to 30 cm) long and a couple of inches in diameter. This is the base of the roulette pipe. The other should be no more than 4 inches (10 cm) long and of a diameter just slightly wider than that of the base pipe. Ideally, it should be of a greater thickness, as will become clear. This will form the revolving barrel. If you are cutting these tubes to size, make lines and **saw** them on those lines to ensure that the ends are completely level. This is vital to the usability of the pipe.

3 Pick up the barrel and, using a **pen**, mark six equally spaced holes around the midsection. Make sure the holes are exactly parallel to the end of the tube.

4 Next, secure the barrel in a **vise** and bore the six holes. The diameter of each of these holes needs to be in proportion to the width of the bowl pipe threads.

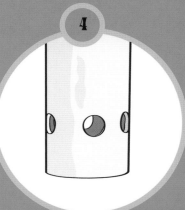

5 Now place the barrel tube flat on a table (with the end with the holes down) and slot the base tube inside it. Using the pen, mark a point on the base tube through any one of the holes on the barrel. Then mark a vertical arrow on the base tube pointing down to the hole. (Of course, with the barrel in place, you will have no way of knowing where it is located otherwise.)

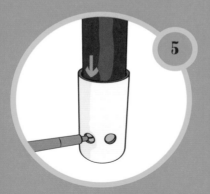

6 Now place the base tube in a vise and **drill** a single hole to the exact dimensions of those on the barrel.

7 Now it's time for the base plate. Cut a piece of **acrylic sheet** about 5 by 5 inches (12 by 12 cm) square. Put the base tube in its center and draw a line around it. Then **glue** around the line.

GAME PLAY

The Roulette pipe makes an excellent addition to your collection of stoner games. You can load the barrels with different substances, introduce forfeits, spin for your neighbor, and more. It provides hours of fun—well, for as long as you're conscious, anyway.

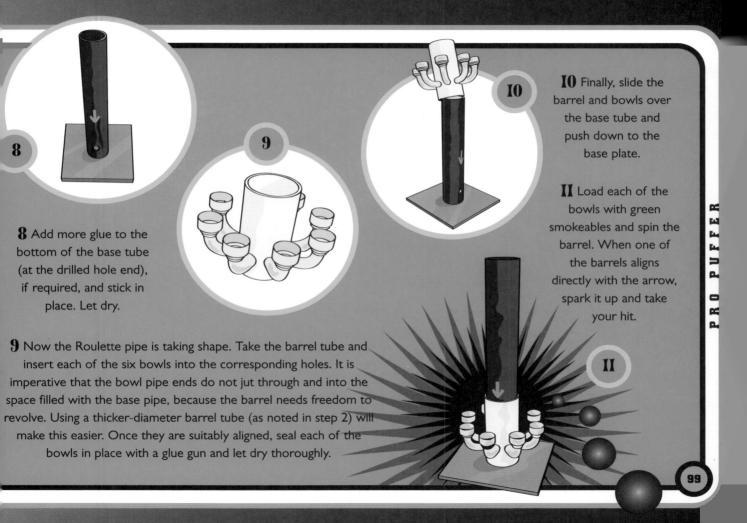

8

8 Add more glue to the bottom of the base tube (at the drilled hole end), if required, and stick in place. Let dry.

9

9 Now the Roulette pipe is taking shape. Take the barrel tube and insert each of the six bowls into the corresponding holes. It is imperative that the bowl pipe ends do not jut through and into the space filled with the base pipe, because the barrel needs freedom to revolve. Using a thicker-diameter barrel tube (as noted in step 2) will make this easier. Once they are suitably aligned, seal each of the bowls in place with a glue gun and let dry thoroughly.

10

10 Finally, slide the barrel and bowls over the base tube and push down to the base plate.

11 Load each of the bowls with green smokeables and spin the barrel. When one of the barrels aligns directly with the arrow, spark it up and take your hit.

11

Deep Freeze

"It's cool, man . . . "

One of the major appeals of any water-based bong is the cooling effect that H$_2$O has on the smoke. And the cooler the smoke, the less abrasive it is on your lungs, and the more pleasurable the hit. It only gets better with the ice bong—as close to silky smooth as you'll ever get. Now you can chill out during and after your smoke.

Hit Power:
※ ※ ※ ※

Freaky Factor:
※ ※ ※ ※

Smoothness:
※ ※ ※ ※

Buildin' Time:
20 minutes

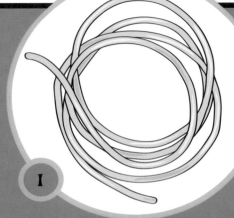

1 This smokeable treat is all about passing the smoke through ice for as long as possible before it reaches the mouthpiece. So first of all you need a large length of clear **vinyl hose**—at least 4 feet, but basically as long as your chamber will hold, with the hose coiled inside.

2 Now take a large, empty beverage **bottle**. Make a hole, large enough to accommodate the vinyl tube, about 4 inches (10 cm) up from the bottom. You can either use a **craft knife** or a burning cigarette.

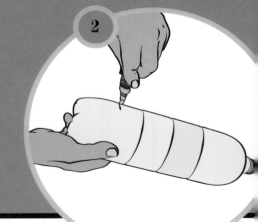

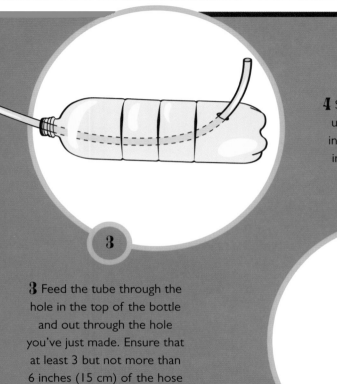

3 Feed the tube through the hole in the top of the bottle and out through the hole you've just made. Ensure that at least 3 but not more than 6 inches (15 cm) of the hose poke through.

4 Seal the tube in position using **duct tape**. Then insert a **bowl** and seal it in place with a **rubber washer** or **putty**.

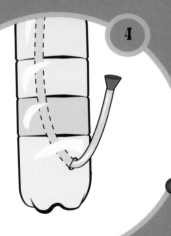

BURN IT UP

A cigarette with a large cherry is an excellent tool for burning tube holes in beverage bottles.

101

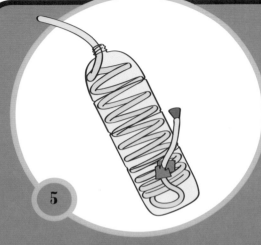

5

6 Raid the refrigerator for as much **ice** as you have. Empty it into a **plastic bag** and smash it into small pieces using a **hammer** or a **rolling pin**. Then add it carefully to the bottle until every vacant crevice is filled with ice.

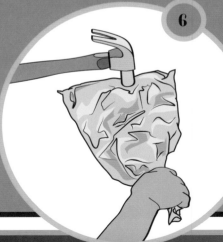

6

7

5 Now carefully start feeding more of the tube into the bottle. The seal at the bowl end will prevent it from pushing through the bottle so it will begin to spiral around inside. Keep feeding the tube into the bottle until it is packed tightly. Make sure that you leave about 6 inches (15 cm) of spare tube at the top of the bottle. This will serve as the mouthpiece.

7 Using a craft knife or similar implement, make a hole in the bottle cap, through which the hose must fit.

8 Feed the cap over the end of the hose and tighten the cap. Add further sealant as required.

8

9 Load the bowl, spark it up, and chill out.

9

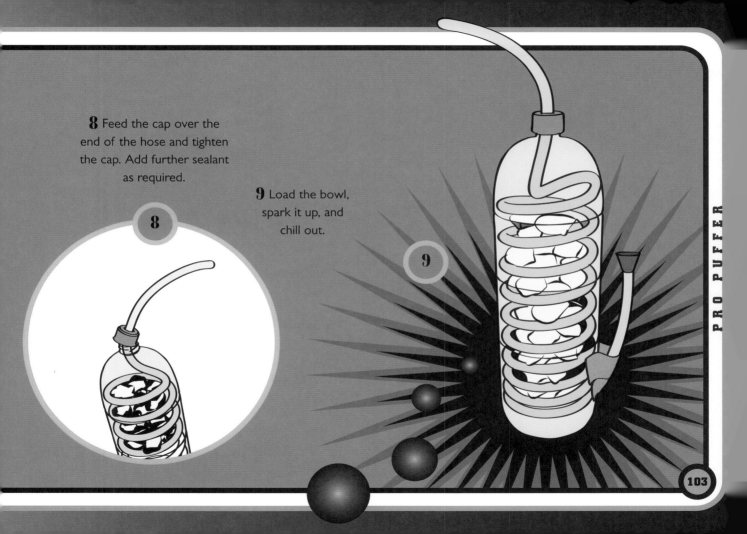

Mini Liquor Bottle Vaporizer

"Heat it up"

Hit Power:
※ ※ ※ ※ ※

Freaky Factor:
※ ※ ※ ※ ※

Smoothness:
※ ※ ※ ※ ※

Buildin' Time:
20 minutes

Store-bought vaporizers are just about the most expensive piece of equipment any stoner can buy. But the principle of heating (not burning) cannabis until it vaporizes is pretty simple. The effect can be achieved using a heating source (a candle) and a sealed glass receptacle, like a lightbulb or small liquor bottle. Just like this:

1 The first step is an added bonus: Drain the contents of a **miniature bottle** of vodka or bourbon. Tasty! Now wash the bottle thoroughly and let dry. It must be bone dry in order to be used as a vaporizer.

2 Screw the cap back onto the bottle and secure the bottle in a **vise**. Then make a small hole (1/8 inch, or 3 mm, in diameter) in the cap with a **drill**.

3 Get a **flexible drinking straw** and cut a piece about 4 inches (10 cm) long to include the flexible section. Discard the rest.

1

2

3

4 Push the straw into the hole and seal along the edge of the straw with **putty**.

5 Unscrew the cap and drop about a joint's worth of weed into the bottle. Retighten the cap.

6 Now hold the bottom of the bottle at least 2 inches (5 cm) above a **candle** flame. When you see a white cloud start to form in the bottle, suck in the vapor. Who says alcohol and pot don't mix?

ILLUMINATING ALTERNATIVE

Sadly, history does not record whether Thomas Edison (1847–1931) was a stoner but if he was he'd surely be delighted at the appropriation of his famous invention for bongologists. The lightbulb vaporizer, which works on a principle that is similar to that of the mini liquor bottle, is a one-hit smoke so it's not for sharing, but the clear view of the smoke buildup is one for the purists.

Stash Box Vaporizer
"Feel the fumes"

Hit Power:
🍁🍁🍁🍁🍁

Freaky Factor:
🍁🍁🍁🍁

Smoothness:
🍁🍁🍁🍁🍁

Buildin' Time:
30 minutes

Every self-respecting stoner owns a stash box, so there's no excuse not to build this vaporizer. There is a little effort required to make the stand—the box (preferably made of tin) containing your weed must be at least **2 inches (5 cm) above the flame in order to keep it from burning**—but it is time well spent to get very pleasantly high.

1 Take a **wire coat hanger** and, using a pair of **wire cutters**, snip off two straight sections about 8 inches (20 cm) long. Take a pair of **pliers** and bend each of the pieces into a U shape, as shown.

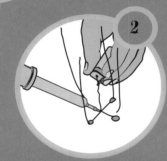

FIZ POP
If you don't have a spare coat hanger or a stash box on hand (shame on you!), don't despair; there is a ready-made solution. The twisted wire cap that seals champagne corks in place is perfect. Simply unwind, flip the cap upside down, and voilà.

2 Upturn the two Us, cross them over at 90 degrees, and seal the edges to the top of a soldering iron box using some **putty**. Now for a task that requires a steady hand (perhaps not something you're known for). Heat up a **soldering iron** and carefully fuse the wire strips together at the cross section point. Let cool.

3 Now take an ordinary **circular stash box** and empty it. Put the lid to one side; you don't need that.

4 With the frame now cooled, take the pliers and bend the four "legs" a little at the bottom so they form "feet." Stand the frame on its feet, place the stash box on top, and add some weed.

5 Now get an empty 2-liter beverage **bottle** (approximately 64 ounces). Keeping the lid in place, remove the bottom portion with a **craft knife** as shown. It's almost time to get vaporizing.

6 Place a small lit **candle** under the frame and place the wide end of the bottle over the frame and tin. When, after a few seconds, you notice the bottle starting to fill with a wispy white cloud (this is the vapor), remove the lid from the bottle and inhale.

Double Bubble

"It's twice the fun"

This twin-chambered device not only looks pretty nifty but is functional too. The smoke is thoroughly cooled by passing through two reservoirs, as opposed to the usual one. You can buy some wonderfully ornate twin-chambered store bongs—if you want to part with $200 (£119)—but my advice would be to build the Double Bubble.

Hit Power:
🟊🟊🟊🟊🟊

Freaky Factor:
🟊🟊🟊🟊🟊

Smoothness:
🟊🟊🟊🟊🟊

Buildin' Time:
45 minutes

1 It's beverage bottle time again, but now on the largest possible scale. You will need two bottles. One should be an empty (and thoroughly rinsed) 5-liter (5 1/4 quart) juice **bottle** (this will act as the first chamber). The second bottle should be a 5-gallon (20 L) **water cooler**. These are not always available in grocery stores, of course, but they are prevalent in offices, and empty ones are often lying around. It's up to you what you do with that information.

2 The essence of this bong is to connect the two bottles and allow smoke to filter through the water in both. The conduit will be a section of **plumbing pipe**. Cut two lengths of this, one about 6 inches (15 cm), the other at least three times that length. These will be connected at an angle via a 90-degree **pipe connector**. All are commonly available at hardware stores. You will also need two 10-inch (25 cm) sections of **vinyl hose**, one to connect to the downpipe of the bowl, the other to act as the mouthpiece.

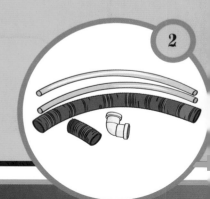

3 Now that you have the pipes sorted out, concentrate on the smaller bottle. Take the 6-inch piece of tubing, put it against the bottle's neck, and mark around its circumference with a **pen**.

4 Then cut around the pen line with a **craft knife**.

5 Now for the burning chamber. Remove the small bottle's lid and make a hole in it that is roughly 1/4 inch (6 mm) in diameter with a craft knife.

6 Next, fix a **bowl and downpipe combo**, available at all good head shops, and make it airtight with a **glue gun** or **putty**.

7 Take a length of flexible vinyl hose about 10 inches (25 cm) long and squeeze it onto the bottom of the downpipe.

8 Finishing off your work on the smaller bottle for the time being, fill it about half full of water and put to one side.

9 Now take hold of the water cooler bottle. Make a hole that is identical in size to the one in the first bottle, just above the halfway point, and a much smaller hole on the opposite side near the neck, through which to add the mouthpiece. Then fill with water to a point just below the first hole.

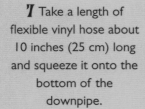

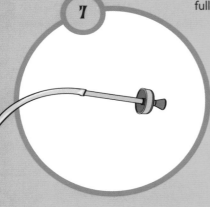

MULTI-STONER USE

This hookah can easily be adapted for multiple person use. Simply add more mouthpieces to the side of the water cooler.

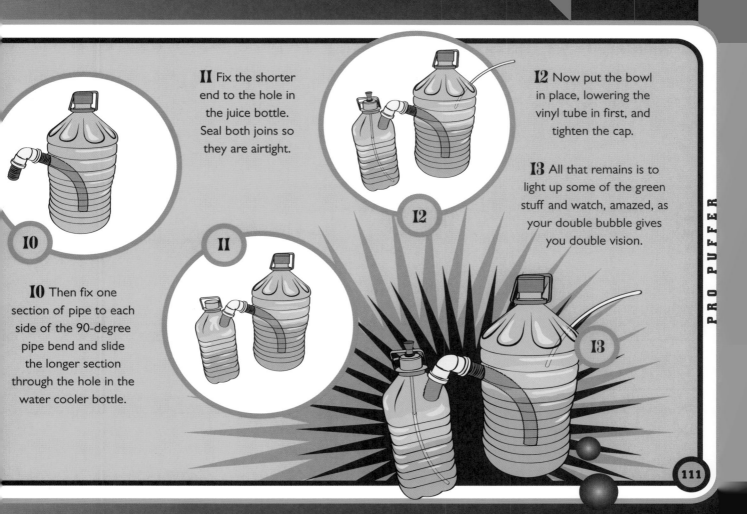

10 Then fix one section of pipe to each side of the 90-degree pipe bend and slide the longer section through the hole in the water cooler bottle.

10

11 Fix the shorter end to the hole in the juice bottle. Seal both joins so they are airtight.

11

12 Now put the bowl in place, lowering the vinyl tube in first, and tighten the cap.

12

13 All that remains is to light up some of the green stuff and watch, amazed, as your double bubble gives you double vision.

13

FAB

"It's electric!"

Hit Power:
🌿🌿🌿🌿🌿

Freaky Factor:
🌿🌿🌿🌿🌿

Smoothness:
🌿🌿🌿🌿🌿

Buildin' Time:
4 hours

When, in the mid-1700s, Benjamin Franklin began pioneering work that would lead to the discovery of electricity, it's likely that he didn't envisage its power being harnessed by stoners 250 years later. Yet the Fan-Assisted Bong does just that—using electrical power to first draw smoke into cooling water, then propel it out, saving your lungs the effort. The ultimate bong for the slacker generation.

I Take a large 5-liter beverage **bottle** (approximately 5 1/4 quarts) and, using a **craft knife**, make two holes approximately 2 inches (5 cm) in diameter—one in the neck, and the other on the opposite side of the bottle about 5 inches (12 cm) up from the base.

2 The basis of the FAB is **electrical fans**. You need two of the small, computer variety—12 volts and about 1 1/2 inches (4 cm) in diameter. (See "Blowin' in the wind," below.)

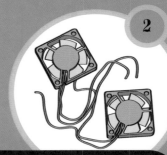

BLOWIN' IN THE WIND

Before you seal either of the fans in place, connect them to an electric source and determine which side exhales the air. This is vital: you don't want to blow the weed out of the bowl or propel smoke away from the mouthpiece!

TIGHT FIT

In time, you will have to fix a downpipe and bowl to either end of the buffer tubes, so, depending on the width of your rubber seals, you may also require two additional pieces of corrugated piping (of a diameter very slightly narrower than that of the tubes) to fit inside. There will be a certain amount of trial and error involved in this process. The end goal is an airtight fit, so any means of achieving this is fine.

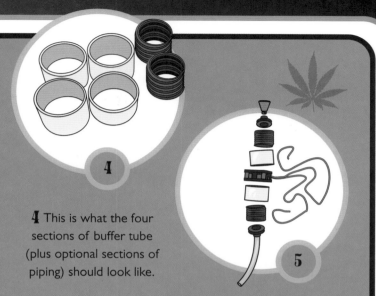

4 This is what the four sections of buffer tube (plus optional sections of piping) should look like.

3 Take a length of **acrylic tubing** of the exact diameter of the fans. Cut four small sections about an inch thick—we'll call these the buffer tubes. Each must be completely level. (See "Tight fit," above.)

5 Take a standard bong **bowl** and place into a **rubber seal**. Then cut a small length (approximately 6 inches/15 cm) of 1/8-inch-diameter (3 mm) **vinyl hose** and fix this around a second rubber seal. The arrangement shown, with the fan in the center, is an "exploded" illustration of the intended end result. Make sure that the extractor side of the fan is facing the bowl, because you want the FAB to suck the air through the ignited weed.

6 Carefully use a **glue gun** to seal every part of the bowl and downpipe combo in place and let dry.

7 Next push the downpipe through the hole in the bottom of the beverage bottle, seal the entry hole with glue, and support the unit with **clear tape**.

8 Now for the mouthpiece. Cut one length of **corrugated tubing** (of a diameter very slightly narrower than that of the tubing in step 3) about 6 inches (15 cm) long, and another about 8 to 10 inches (20 to 25 cm) long. Insert each halfway into the remaining two buffer tubes, glue in place, and allow to dry.

9 Then place the other fan between the buffer tubes (extractor side facing the shortest end) and carefully glue in place once more. Let dry.

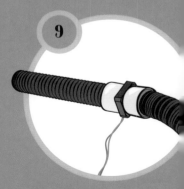

10 Push the shorter end of the mouthpiece into the hole in the neck of the bottle, use a glue gun to make the seal airtight, and let dry. The FAB is starting to look, well, fab.

11 Now to fill the chamber with water. Use a **jug**—at this point you don't want to have to maneuver the fairly cumbersome unit to a tap. Make sure the water is well above the downpipe but below the mouthpiece.

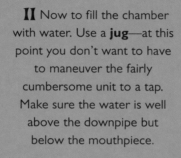

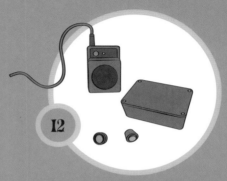

12 Now for the power! To operate the fans you will need a low voltage **AC adapter**, a few inches of **live** and **neutral electric wire** (this will probably come with the adapter), a **junction box** and **switches**, and a **soldering iron**.

BONGOLOGY

13 First, remove the lid from the junction box and glue the bottom to the side of the beverage bottle. Allow to dry.

13

14 Cut two lengths of **vinyl hose** to encase the wires. One fan is positioned closer to the junction box than the other, so measure roughly to determine the length of each.

15

14

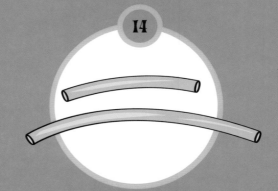

15 Take the wires of one of the fans and pass them through the vinyl tube. Repeat for the wires of the other fan.

DON'T GET STUCK

Since the FAB features so many intricate parts, gluing is vital. However, be wary of gluing to excess. Not only will the finished design look unsightly, but more importantly if any glue seeps onto the fan blades the mechanism won't work.

116

16 Pass both sets of wires through the hole at the top of the junction box. Trim the length if necessary, seal the ends in place, and put the bong to one side.

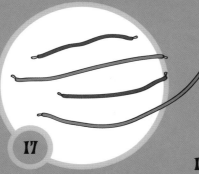

17 Now cut and strip the ends of two lengths of red (live) and two black (neutral) electric wire. Each strip should be about 4 inches (10 cm) long.

18 Twist one end of both the neutral strips around the neutral wire of the AC adapter . . .

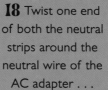

19 . . . and carefully solder these in place.

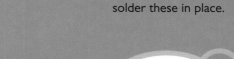

20 Repeat for the live wires.

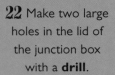

21 Feed the two V-shaped ends through the hole in the bottom of the junction box.

22 Make two large holes in the lid of the junction box with a **drill**.

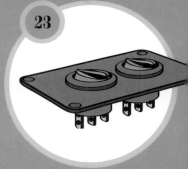

23 Slot the switches in place and seal.

SAFETY FIRST

Needless to say, any electrical work (despite the low voltage of this project) should be undertaken with extreme care—especially where water is present. The fans are simple to wire up, but if you are in any doubt consult a professional—you don't have to tell him what you're using the fans for.

24 Now connect the eight separate wires to the appropriate terminals on the underside of the switches (these will be labeled). Use the soldering iron to seal these in place.

25 Carefully push all of the wires inside the box and tighten the lid with screws.

26 Now all that remains is to add some weed to the bowl, light it, turn on the fans, and prepare to be amazed.

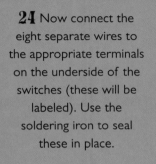

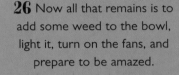

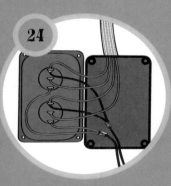

Other ideas to try ... and get high

Sadly there hasn't been room in this tome for me to feature every device I've ever made. But here's a trio of ideas to keep you going when you've exhausted every other project in this book—from the sublime to the faintly ridiculous.

Hot Knives
"Flaming good"

A student favorite, hot knives is a hassle-free means of ingesting weed. All you need are two **dinner knives**, a plastic **bottle** (minus the lower portion), and access to a naked **flame**. Oh, and some pot, of course. Get a buddy to compress a nugget of hash between two knife blades over the flame. As the smoke rises, position your bottle over the plume and inhale deeply.

The Chillum
"Holy smoke!"

A pipe of religious significance for Indian Sadhus and Rastafarians, the chillum is conical in shape and is made of either clay, cow's horn, glass, stone, or wood. The chillum is hollow and also loaded with grass. Consequently, the hit from one of these mothers is something of truly biblical proportions. So, with some classic Marley on the sound system, offer your praises to Haile Selassie and hang on tight.

VEGETABLE CHILLUM
For an alternative smoke, why not hollow out a large carrot and use that?

The Cistern
"The bathroom bong"

This one is only to be utilized when you are truly desperate for a novel hit, because it causes permanent damage to your **toilet cistern**. First, make the cistern lid airtight. Then **drill** a hole in the top wide enough to accommodate a **bowl**. Load with weed, light, and simultaneously flush. As the water falls into the toilet bowl, the smoke is drawn down. When the toilet's finished flushing, remove the bowl, put your mouth over the hole, and wait as the smoke is pushed up and into your mouth. Anyone crazy enough to embrace The Cistern shall be fêted as a top bongologist.

chapter 5

PIMP MY BONG!

"I didn't give a shit she got my first name wrong
She only wants me for my Bucket Bong"

Frenzal Rhomb, "Bucket Bong"

Now that you're a full-fledged bongology grad, you can turn your attention to aesthetics. Why stick with a smoking device with a prosaic appearance when you can paint, glaze, sticker, and otherwise embellish it? Adding that personal touch will make all the difference and ensure that your bong is the envy of your smoking circle.

Rocket Man

"The big blast off"

You'll need a mastery of the potter's wheel before you tackle this project (see "Clay Bongs") but the rewards of doing so are self-evident. Once made, fired, glazed, and pimped to excess all that remains is to load the bowl. The effects of a few blasts on this monster will transport you (mentally, if not physically) to outer space. So take a deep breath and prepare for takeoff.

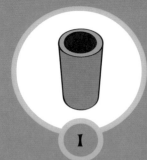

1 Take a chunk of **modeling clay**. How much you use depends on the dimensions of the rocket you want to create. Now shape that clay into a hollow cylinder—the fuselage. This can be accomplished either with your nimble fingers on the wheel or with an "extruder"—a machine that does this for you.

2 Now take the bottom of the cylinder, place it on a new flattened piece of clay, and score around the edge. Cut this to size, pat with water, and smooth around the edges to create a base that is bonded to the cylinder.

3 Make a small hole about 1/2 inch (12 mm) in diameter about 6 inches (15 cm) up from the base. This will be used to house the bowl and downpipe.

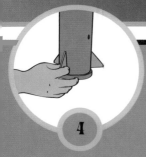

4 Make the wings: cut four identical triangular shapes. Space them equally around the circumference of the cylinder, as shown, and seal them in place.

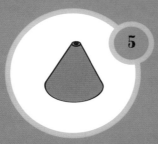

5 Make the nosecone: mold a pyramid-shaped cone, with a narrow opening at the top. Seal the bottom onto the top of the cylinder.

6 Now your rocket is headed for the **kiln**. You will first need to "biscuit" your bong (fire it at a temperature lower than normal in preparation for glazing). Once completed, glaze the outside of the bong with your chosen color, and then fire it again.

7 Add a **bowl and downpipe combo** to the side hole. Finally, using **paint** specially formulated for clay, decorate your rocket with the pattern of your choice, such as this large marijuana leaf and NASA (National American Stoners' Association) logo.

NASA

CLAY BONGS

Potting, or the art of working with clay, is a specialized skill that is beyond the scope of the average bongologist. However, clay is highly malleable and air- and watertight once fired, so it's a great material to use as a bong. Plus, it lends itself perfectly to pimping with paint or glaze. Enroll yourself in a class soon and embrace the magic of the potter's wheel.

GLAZING

Glaze the outside of your bong only—never the inside.

Other Pimping Ideas

What do you do when you've (heaven forbid) run out of bongs, pipes, and hookahs to make? Start pimping up your existing ones, that's what. There are various ways to embellish the smoking contraptions you've made in the chapters of this book. Here are a few ideas to get you started. Get inspired and get crafting.

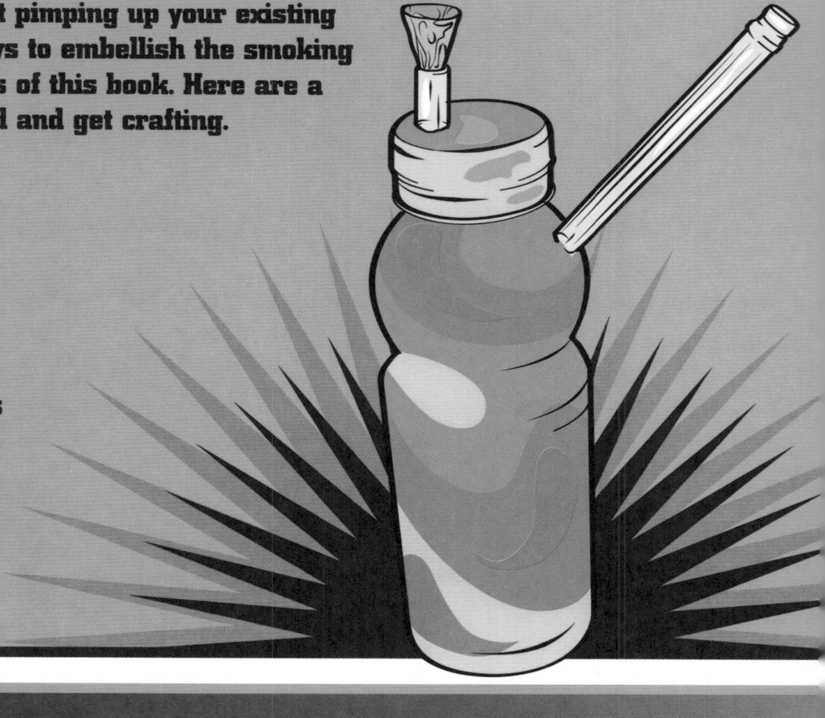

Painting

One option is to decorate your smoking device with different kinds of paint, in a multitude of designs. Try horizontal or vertical stripes; a wild palette for a 1960s psychedelic look; fluorescent paint for the glow-in-the-dark vibe; the Acid House smiley face; or, if you're feeling patriotic, even stars and stripes. Michelangelo you ain't, but you gotta start somewhere.

BONGOLOGY

126

WARNING: TOXIC FUMES

Stickers

Just like they do on a pimped skate- or surfboard, stickers make a great addition to any homemade bong. Of course, there's a particular worldwide surfing brand whose logos are widely available—and the name says it all! And your local hardware store most likely stocks a range of great stickers. Try "Radioactive," "Danger!" "Keep Out!" or, most pertinently, "Warning: Toxic Fumes."

Power up

For an automotive angle, why not paint your bong with classic "go-faster" racing stripes? You could craft yourself an exhaust unit from a bunch of cut-down drinking straws sprayed silver and bound together. But, best of all, make some intricate circles out of tin foil and fix yourself some mean-lookin' alloys.

Happy birthday to ya

If you're planning a bong as a gift, say for a friend's birthday, why not festoon your chamber with sparkly lights? Then, for the pièce de résistance, cram a big juicy bud in the mouthpiece and stick a lit candle in it. Now that's a present worthy of any stoner. Remind me to give you my address so you can mail me one.

ACKNOWLEDGMENTS

It seems like only yesterday that I was putting the finishing touches to my last literary masterpiece, *Spliffigami*. In fact . . . perhaps it was yesterday; it's easy to lose track of time when you smoke as much as I do.

To get a repeat commission to mess about for six months making cannabis contraptions and smoking them has obviously been a delight. Long may these books continue! Thanks go once again to Will Steeds and Laura Ward at Elephant Book Company for getting me the gig; to Ten Speed Press for supporting counterculture; to Lindsey Johns for another great layout; to Rob Brandt for making sense of my photographs to produce some killer illustrations; and especially to Paul Malden (aka P. Malden Esq., aka Paulo Maldonas) for his invaluable help at every stage of the creative process—he is a true bongologist. I couldn't have done it without you, man.